Scalable Artificial Intelligence for Healthcare

This edited volume examines the transformative impact of AI technologies on global healthcare systems, with a focus on enhancing efficiency and accessibility. The content provides a comprehensive exploration of the principles and practices required to scale AI applications in healthcare, addressing areas such as diagnosis, treatment, and patient care. Key topics include data scalability, model deployment, and infrastructure design, highlighting the use of microservices, containerization, cloud computing, and big data technologies in building scalable AI systems. Discussions cover advancements in machine learning models, distributed processing, and transfer learning, alongside critical considerations such as continuous integration, data privacy, and ethics. Real-world case studies depict both the successes and challenges of implementing scalable AI across various healthcare environments, offering valuable insights for future advancements. This volume serves as a practical and theoretical guide for healthcare professionals, AI researchers, and technology enthusiasts seeking to develop or expand on AI-driven healthcare solutions to address global health challenges effectively.

Houneida Sakly is an Assistant Professor at CRMN in Tunisia's Sousse Techno Park. Holding a Ph.D. from ENSI in partnership with French universities (Gustave Eiffel University—ESIEE Paris and Polytech Orléans), she specializes in data science applied to healthcare. She collaborates with Stanford and is certified by MIT–Harvard in healthcare innovation.

Ramzi Guetari is an Associate Professor of Computer Science at the Polytechnic School of Tunisia. He achieved his Ph.D. at the University of Savoie, France, worked at the INRIA, contributed to W3C standards, and now studies AI and machine learning, collaborating with international organizations and companies.

Naoufel Kraiem is a Full Professor of Computer Science with 32 years in academia. He earned his Ph.D. at the University of Paris 6 and Habilitation from Sorbonne University. His research spans IT, data science, and software engineering, supported by the CNRS, INRIA, and EU programs, with over 147 publications.

Analytics and AI for Healthcare

Artificial Intelligence (AI) and analytics are increasingly being applied to various healthcare settings. AI and analytics are salient to facilitate better understanding and identifying key insights from healthcare data in many areas of practice and enquiry including at the genomic, individual, hospital, community and/or population levels. The Chapman&Hall/CRC Press Analytics and AI in Healthcare Series aims to help professionals upskill and leverage the techniques, tools, technologies and tactics of analytics and AI to achieve better healthcare delivery, access, and outcomes. The series covers all areas of analytics and AI as applied to healthcare. It will look at critical areas including prevention, prediction, diagnosis, treatment, monitoring, rehabilitation and survivorship.

ABOUT THE SERIES EDITOR

Professor Nilmini Wickramasinghe is Professor of Digital Health and the Deputy Director of the Iverson Health Innovation Research Institute at Swinburne University of Technology, Australia and is inaugural Professor – Director Health Informatics Management at Epworth HealthCare, Victoria, Australia. She also holds honorary research professor positions at the Peter MacCallum Cancer Centre, Murdoch Children's Research Institute and Northern Health. For over 20 years, Professor Wickramasinghe has been researching and teaching within the health informatics/digital health domain. She was awarded the prestigious Alexander von Humboldt award in recognition of her outstanding contribution to digital health.

Dimensions of Intelligent Analytics for Smart Digital Health Solutions
Edited by Nilmini Wickramasinghe, Freimut Bodendorf and Mathias Kraus

Digital Health
A Primer
Nilmini Wickramasinghe

Using Blockchain Technology in Healthcare Settings
Empowering Patients with Trustworthy Data
Edited by Ben Othman Soufiene, Saurav Mallik and Abdulatif Alabdulatif

Modern Technologies in Healthcare
AI, Computer Vision, Robotics
Edited by Temitope Emmanuel Komolafe, Patrice Monkam, Blessing Funmi Komolafe and Nizhuan Wang

Scalable Artificial Intelligence for Healthcare
Advancing AI Solutions for Global Health Challenges
Edited by Houneida Sakly, Ramzi Guetari and Naoufel Kraiem

For more information about this series please visit: https://www.routledge.com/analytics-and-ai -for-healthcare/book-series/Aforhealth

Scalable Artificial Intelligence for Healthcare
Advancing AI Solutions for Global Health Challenges

Edited by Houneida Sakly, Ramzi Guetari, and Naoufel Kraiem

CRC Press
Taylor & Francis Group
Boca Raton London New York

CRC Press is an imprint of the
Taylor & Francis Group, an **informa** business

Designed cover image: Blue Caduceus Hologram Over Robotic Hands Cyber Medicine Concept High-Res Stock Photo – Getty Images

First edition published 2025
by CRC Press
2385 NW Executive Center Drive, Suite 320, Boca Raton FL 33431

and by CRC Press
4 Park Square, Milton Park, Abingdon, Oxon, OX14 4RN

CRC Press is an imprint of Taylor & Francis Group, LLC

ISBN: [978-1-032-76960-8] (hbk)
ISBN: [978-1-032-76959-2] (pbk)
ISBN: [978-1-003-48059-4] (ebk)

DOI: 10.1201/9781003480594

Typeset in Sabon
by Deanta Global Publishing Services, Chennai, India

Contents

Editor Biographies

Houneida Sakly is an Assistant Professor of Informatics at the Center for Research in Microelectronics & Nanotechnology (CRMN) in the technopark of Sousse, Tunisia, and a researcher within RIADI laboratory. She received her Ph.D. in Computer Science from the National School of Computer Science (ENSI) within Manouba University in 2019 in collaboration with Gustave Eiffel University—ESIEE Paris and Polytech Orléans engineering faculty. In addition, she is a member of the research program "deep learning analysis of radiologic imaging" at Stanford University. She is certified in Healthcare Innovation with MIT-Harvard Medical School. Her main field of research is data science (Artificial Intelligence, Big Data, blockchain, Internet of Things, etc.) applied in healthcare. She is a member of the Integrated Science Association (ISA) in the Universal Scientific Education and Research Network (USERN) in Tunisia. Currently, she is serving as a lead editor for various books, conferences, and special issues in the fields of digital transformation and data science in healthcare. Recently, she won the Best Researcher Award at the International Conference on Cardiology and Cardiovascular Medicine in San Francisco, United States. Currently, she is recognized as an academic instructor (HCIA) with Huawei in artificial intelligence and cloud computing.

Ramzi Guetari is an Associate Professor in Computer Science at the Polytechnic School of Tunisia. He obtained his Ph.D. in Computer Science from the University of "Savoie" in France and worked as a Research Engineer at the National Institute for Research in Computer Science and Control (INRIA), where he was seconded to the Worldwide Web Consortium (W3C). He participated in the development and promotion of web technologies and notably participated in the development of Amaya, the W3C test bed. He was at the origin of the internationalization of Amaya. For more than ten years, Ramzi has been working in the industrial field and has led large-scale missions for international organizations such as WIPO and WMO, as well as for important companies such as NESTLE, NOVARTIS, ABN AMRO BANK, and CAP GEMINI. Ramzi's research has focused on distributed information systems and fundamental computing. For more than a decade, he has been working on artificial intelligence, particularly machine learning.

He has obtained a number of certifications in this area from MIT, Harvard University, and IBM and has supervised Ph.D. work in this area.

Naoufel Kraiem is a Full Professor of Computer Science at the College of Computer Science, with over 32 years of experience in academia. He obtained his B.S. in Computer Science from the University of Sfax in 1988, followed by an M.S. from the University of Toulouse in 1990. He earned his Ph.D. in Computer Science from the University of Paris 6 in 1995 and later achieved his Habilitation in Computer Science from Sorbonne University (Paris 1) in 2011. His research interests are diverse, spanning IT adoption and usage, information modeling, software engineering, software product lines, requirements engineering, data science, and CASE tools. His work has been supported by prestigious funding bodies, including CNRS, INRIA, and the Ministry of Research, Technology, and Industry, as well as by the Commission of the European Communities under the ESPRIT Programs (BUSINESS CLASS) and UNIDO (National Network of Industrial Information Project). Professor Kraiem has delivered invited talks and presentations across North America, Europe, Africa, and the Middle East, sharing his insights into these topics. His contributions include over 147 publications and presentations in leading international journals and conferences, and he has served on more than 35 program committees.

Contributor Biographies

Mourad Abed is a Full Professor of Computer Engineering, earned his Ph.D. in Computer Science in 1990 and completed a Habilitation to direct research at UVHC in 2001. He has served as Deputy Director and Director of the Master Cycle at ISTV, overseeing "technological innovations" and "digital" initiatives at UVHC. His research is conducted within the LAMIH UMR CNRS 8201 Research in Computer Science Department where he is also a team member. Professor Abed has supervised Ph.D. theses and Habilitations to Direct Research both in France and Tunisia and is actively involved in various research groups, as well as scientific committees for journals and conferences. He founded the ICALT conference and has led numerous research projects with major corporations (Peugeot, CENA, EuroCopter, SNCF) and national and European programs (ANR, PREDIT, Tempus, Erasmus+). With over 150 publications in international journals and conferences, as well as books and research reports, his expertise spans intelligent interactive and decision support systems, information retrieval, and logistics systems.

Ahmed Wajdi Abdallah holds a Ph.D. in Computer Science from ENSI and a Master's degree in Software Engineering from the Higher Institute of Computer Science and Mathematics of Monastir (2021–2023). His research focuses on IoT cybersecurity in radiology, utilizing quantum AI and large language models (LLMs) to enhance medical imaging security.

Alaeddine Behmida holds a Ph.D. in Computer Science from ENSI and a Master's degree in Software Engineering from the Higher Institute of Computer Science and Mathematics of Monastir (2021–2023). His research explores quantum learning and large language models (LLMs) as innovative approaches for personalized medicine in chronic disease prevention.

Mourad Said, M.D. has been an Associate Professor in Radiology and Medical Imaging since 2002. He is a member of the regional committee Africa–Middle East of the Radiological Society of North America (RSNA) (2014–2018). He has been an author and reviewer for the prestigious journal *Radiology* for many years. He has delivered various scientific presentations at RSNA meetings. He is board-certified in MRI from South Paris University. He also has qualifications in Pediatric/Obstetric Radiology and MSK Imaging. He is currently interested in artificial intelligence in medical imaging, deep learning, and radiomics, with different publications.

1 AI in Healthcare
Addressing Challenges and Enabling Transformation

Houneida Sakly, Ramzi Guetari,
Naoufel Kraiem, and Mourad Said

1. Introduction

The diagnosis is accurate, treatments are tailored to specific patient needs, and administrative procedures are improved to enhance efficiency, ensuring optimal patient care and administrative effectiveness. Given that developed AI applications need to be implemented from the laboratory to actual healthcare practice, the concept of scalability is important. A crucial word. The simplest definition of scalability is being able to increase the amount of data, the size of the network, or the complexity of the tasks the AI system is capable of performing. The AI system can accomplish this task with the same, or even better, level of productivity and efficiency. In the context of global healthcare systems, evolution is not limited to technological aspects but is also a highly complex issue encompassing legal, ethical, and infrastructural aspects. These are legal, ethical, and infrastructural issues (Alandjani, 2023; Shende, 2022). Healthcare presents a specific challenge for the evolution of AI due to the complexity of the sector itself. The disparities between information, types of care, and patient populations in different regions and institutions indicate that AI requires systems that are flexible enough to adapt to different environments without compromising their effectiveness. Moreover, healthcare data are sensitive and require stringent confidentiality and security protocols, which limits the evolution of AI solutions. As a result, it is difficult for healthcare establishments to strike a balance between making optimal use of AI and complying with regulations designed to safeguard the well-being of individuals (Chidi & Odimba, 2024). Furthermore, the adaptability of AI in healthcare is closely linked to the availability and quality of information. High-quality, representative datasets are crucial for designing AI models that can be applied to all patient populations (*Ethical Considerations in AI-Enabled Big Data Research: Balancing Innovation and Privacy*, 2020; Ness et al., 2024). However, data storage systems and fragmented medical records frequently hinder the flow of information essential to the evolution of AI. To remedy these data problems, not only technological advances but also collaboration between healthcare players to establish interoperable systems and data-sharing agreements are needed (Arigbabu et al., 2024; Peixoto et al., 2016).

DOI: 10.1201/9781003480594-1

This paper analyzes the challenges involved in AI scalability in the context of the current healthcare situation and discusses its main pain points. The paper aims to present a wide view of approaches to scaling AI in practice and how technologies can be developed to realize those approaches through case studies. In the end, the analysis of future prospects will provide insight into ways of resolving these challenges, promoting the integration of AI in improving healthcare systems worldwide.

2.1 Understanding AI Scalability in Healthcare

Scalability in healthcare is about extending artificial intelligence systems to handle more data and users without losing speed or accuracy. As the healthcare field generates increasing amounts of data, it is crucial to develop AI systems efficiently. This ensures that AI tools remain useful in a variety of situations, from small clinics to large hospital infrastructures. A major challenge in making AI scalable in healthcare lies in combining various types of data from different sources. Healthcare data often come from a variety of places and formats, such as electronic health records, imaging tools, and wearable devices. To effectively extend artificial intelligence solutions, it is essential to design systems that can easily gather and analyze all these different types of data (Agafonov et al., 2024; Aljabri, 2022; Dhawan & Kumar, 2024; Haleem, 2021).

In addition, the ethical and legal issues associated with the use of AI in healthcare make the adoption of these systems more difficult. It is essential to protect patient privacy and data security, which requires solid rules and systems that respect the law and enable the evolution of artificial intelligence. These rules guarantee not only data protection but also the transparency and accountability of AI systems when they are used more generally. AI has considerable potential to transform healthcare by making diagnoses more accurate, personalizing treatments, and optimizing the use of resources. AI has the ability to analyze large quantities of data to identify patterns and trends that humans might overlook, facilitating early detection and preventive care. In healthcare, companies need to have the right technologies in place, such as cloud computing and powerful IT systems (Hoseini, 2023).

Artificial intelligence scalability is an essential element in healthcare, meaning that artificial intelligence systems can handle more tasks or develop their skills over time. AI systems are capable of handling larger amounts of data and various types of data, which is common in healthcare. The key elements influencing scalability are computing resources and system design. Unlike older systems, artificial intelligence has to cope with complex data patterns and learn from them. Ensuring the scalability of AI systems has a direct effect on their performance and efficiency, which is essential for the successful use of AI in healthcare (Ness et al., 2024; Palaniappan et al., 2024).

When considering the development of AI in healthcare, it is essential to consider its integration with the current healthcare system and the new capabilities it can bring. The key to the successful implementation of AI in healthcare lies in its ability to integrate seamlessly with current systems and day-to-day tasks. It is crucial to ensure the effective use of AI tools without disrupting current healthcare practices. In addition, AI systems designed to scale must be built to maintain their performance as they develop. This means not only processing more data but also handling more complex calculations. The design of these systems generally relies on cloud-based services and cloud computing, which offer the flexibility and power needed to process and analyze large-scale data. By using these technologies, healthcare providers can guarantee the robustness and efficiency of their artificial intelligence systems, even as their range of patients or complex data increases (Babarinde et al., 2023). Moreover, it is crucial to be able to extend artificial intelligence in healthcare to reduce disparities in access to healthcare. Through the use of scalable AI solutions, healthcare providers can extend their services to regions where access to healthcare is limited, offering assistance in decision-making (Agafonov et al., 2024; Dhawan & Kumar 2024; Haleem, 2021). In addition to increasing access, scalable artificial intelligence systems contribute to better personalized healthcare. As more data are collected, artificial intelligence can offer personalized treatment suggestions and patterns that might be invisible via full-fledged human analysis. This personalized approach improves patient outcomes and gives them more control by involving them more in their treatment choices. Finally, scalability plays an essential role in the continuous improvement of AI models. As these systems face new data and situations, scalable AI can learn and adapt, improving its algorithms to increase their accuracy, as shown in Table 1.1.

3.1. Challenges of Scaling AI in Healthcare

3.1.1 Technical Challenges

A major challenge in using artificial intelligence in healthcare is coping with all the rules and standards. This list includes the rules of the Health Insurance Portability and Accountability Act (HIPAA) and the Food and Drug Administration (FDA). It is essential to pay close attention and comply with these rules. These regulations are designed to safeguard patient safety and confidentiality, but they can also make the use and expansion of artificial intelligence technology more difficult and slower. In addition, it is essential to consider workforce readiness for the use of AI tools. Healthcare workers must be adequately trained to understand and work effectively with AI systems. This involves creating education and training sessions that equip healthcare providers with the necessary skills and knowledge. Otherwise, the integration of artificial intelligence into everyday healthcare tasks may encounter obstacles or lead to less effective use (Roppelt et al., 2024). Collaboration with different groups is crucial when dealing with issues that make growth or expansion difficult. This involves collaboration between individuals who create

Table 1.1 Summary of published papers related to AI and healthcare

Reference	Techniques	Objective	Findings	Challenges	Data
Nahavandi, D., et al. (2022). "Application of artificial intelligence in wearable devices: Opportunities and challenges." *Computer Methods and Programs in Biomedicine* (Nahavandi, et al, 2022).	AI-powered wearable devices for patient monitoring; predictive analytics for disease prevention.	Integrating AI into routine clinical workflows while ensuring privacy and regulatory compliance.	AI-powered wearables improve patient monitoring and preventive care.	Privacy risks, lack of proper regulatory frameworks.	Wearable device data, patient health records.
Schork, N. J., (2019). "Artificial intelligence and personalized medicine." *Cancer Treatment and Research* (Schork, 2019).	Machine learning for genomic data analysis; AI for personalized treatment recommendations.	Developing AI models that can effectively personalize treatment plans based on genomic and clinical data.	AI enables personalized treatment plans, improving outcomes for various conditions.	High computational demands, privacy concerns.	Genomic data, clinical records.
Kolasa, K., et al. (2023). "Systematic reviews of machine learning in healthcare: A literature review." *Expert Review of Pharmacoeconomics & Outcomes Research* (Kolasa, K., et al, 2023).	Deep learning, reinforcement learning, unsupervised machine learning for diagnostic applications.	Improving the accuracy of AI diagnostic tools in healthcare.	AI-driven diagnostics improve early detection and treatment effectiveness.	Algorithm bias, ethical concerns.	Medical diagnostic datasets, EHRs.
(Haleem, A., et al. (2021). "Blockchain technology applications in healthcare: An overview." *International Journal of Intelligent Networks* (Haleem, 2021)	AI combined with blockchain for secure healthcare data sharing.	Addressing the privacy and security risks associated with healthcare data management.	AI-blockchain integration enhances data privacy, security, and interoperability in healthcare.	Regulatory challenges, high costs.	Medical data, blockchain frameworks.

Reference					
Panayides, A. S., et al. (2020). "AI in medical imaging informatics: Current challenges and future directions." *IEEE Journal of Biomedical and Health Informatics* (Panayides, et al., 2020).	Deep learning algorithms for medical image analysis; AI for image segmentation and classification.	AI models in medical imaging, data quality, and model interpretability.	AI significantly improves accuracy and speed in medical image analysis.	Limited interpretability of deep learning models.	Medical imaging datasets (CT, MRI, X-ray).
Naik, B., et al, (2022). "Legal and Ethical Consideration in Artificial Intelligence in Healthcare: Who Takes Responsibility?." *Front Surg* (Naik, 2022).	AI in legal frameworks, policy analysis.	Ethical dilemmas and legal barriers in AI implementation in healthcare.	Proposes legal reforms and ethical guidelines to regulate AI in healthcare.	Lack of comprehensive legal frameworks.	—
White, et al. (2014). "A review of big data in health care: challenges and opportunities." *Open Access Bioinformatics* (White, 2014).	Data mining and analytics techniques for healthcare data.	The need for effective data management strategies.	Improved patient outcomes and healthcare efficiencies through data insights.	Data quality issues and integration challenges.	Electronic health records, patient surveys.

technology, doctors, government leaders, and patients. Integrating different teams ensures that artificial intelligence tools work properly and meet the needs and desires of the healthcare industry. It is also essential to think about what is fair and equitable to build trust and help people accept artificial intelligence tools. Ensuring that AI decisions are clear and that someone is accountable for the results is essential to encourage the evolution and increasing use of AI. Finally, making healthcare AI projects sustainable means taking into account their impact on the environment, particularly in regard to storing and processing data. As AI systems develop and become more data-driven, their energy consumption can be very high. It is crucial to design energy-efficient AI models and use environmentally friendly technologies to ensure that the expansion of AI does not harm the environment. It's not just about improving technology in healthcare. It requires a great deal of work in various areas, such as compliance with rules, training employees, collaborating with others, taking justice into account, and preserving the environment. All these factors are crucial for artificial intelligence to transform the way healthcare works (White, 2014; Naik, 2022; Panayides 2020).

3.1.2   Ethical and privacy concerns

In the field of healthcare AI scalability, the preservation of patient data is highly important because of the increased risk of data breaches and unauthorized access. It is essential that AI decisions are transparent and comprehensive to maintain trust, especially when dealing with biases that could negatively impact patient care. It is essential to prioritize consent and control over data collection and use, in line with regulations such as GDPR and HIPAA. It is vital to reconcile innovation and ethical considerations to reduce the impact of artificial intelligence errors on patient safety. It is crucial to establish ethical guidelines to safeguard patients' rights and address concerns about data ownership (Palaniappan et al., 2024).

3.1.3   Regulatory and Compliance Issues

The use of AI in healthcare is heavily influenced by rules and guidelines that establish legal and ethical boundaries for the use of these technologies. Compliance with these rules is essential to ensure the proper functioning of AI systems, which means having an understanding of data protection laws such as GDPR and HIPAA. This legislation includes stringent rules to ensure total clarity and accountability, but it can be difficult to comply with them when creating artificial intelligence systems. Ethical issues play a crucial role in these rules, helping create plans for dealing with the challenges of complying with them. Looking at what has and has not worked before can provide ideas about what will happen in the future, highlighting the constant evolution of the rules for artificial intelligence and their impact on new ideas in healthcare (Tothy et al., 2016).

3.1.4 *Integration with Existing Systems*

Integrating artificial intelligence into today's healthcare systems is crucial to improving patient care and operations. However, it can be difficult to integrate artificial intelligence into older systems. It is essential to share data effectively and ensure that different systems can collaborate, and the use of APIs helps with this. This has an impact on the fluidity of operations and requires particular attention to preserving data security and confidentiality. Training and support for healthcare workers are needed to facilitate change. Examples of successful integration show that while there may be costs involved, long-term benefits such as the opportunity to develop and innovate are significant (Wang et al., 2012).

4.1 Technological Solutions for AI Scalability

4.1.1 *Cloud Computing and AI*

Moreover, as healthcare systems increasingly rely on cloud computing, the ability of different healthcare platforms to collaborate seamlessly is greatly enhanced. The ability to collaborate is essential to facilitate the sharing of information between different healthcare providers and systems, helping to improve patient care. By using cloud-based solutions, healthcare organizations can make effective use of artificial intelligence across various compartments and locations, ensuring consistent and well-coordinated healthcare delivery. Indeed, the effective growth of artificial intelligence applications also relies on sound data management strategies. Given that healthcare generates a great deal of data every day, managing this information is a complex task. Cloud computing offers scalable methods for storing and processing data, making it easier for healthcare centers to manage large datasets. This makes it possible to combine different data sources, such as electronic health records, imaging data, and genetic information, which are essential for in-depth artificial intelligence analysis.

Moreover, the use of cloud computing in healthcare AI scalability is driven by the need for flexibility and rapid response. As healthcare needs evolve, so must the AI applications that support them. The cloud offers the opportunity to test new models of artificial intelligence and algorithms without the need for large upfront investments in physical infrastructure. This adaptability is essential in the ever-changing healthcare field, where the ability to respond rapidly to new healthcare challenges or changing patient populations can have significant consequences.

Moreover, cloud computing helps make artificial intelligence in healthcare accessible to smaller companies that might not have the financial resources to develop large-scale IT systems. This facilitates access to advanced technologies, encouraging the emergence of new ideas and competition. It encourages the creation of innovative artificial intelligence tools capable of solving unique healthcare problems. By facilitating the use of AI by an increasing number of healthcare providers, cloud platforms help improve patient care, making care more personalized and efficient (Singh & Singh, 2024; Wang et al., 2012).

4.1.2 Interoperability Standards

Interoperability standards are essential rules and methods for ensuring that different digital systems and software can communicate and collaborate harmoniously. These standards are highly important in the healthcare field, as they enable the easy exchange of information between different platforms and organizations. By making this sharing possible, interoperability standards help improve patient care, reduce errors, and make care delivery more efficient. They also contribute to the expansion of AI technologies by ensuring that new innovations can be easily incorporated into existing systems, which allows for greater usage and a greater impact (Kesan & Shah, 2008). Interoperability standards (Wang et al., 2012) are essential in the field of medical artificial intelligence, enabling the smooth flow of data across different systems. Standards such as HL7 and FHIR play a crucial role in accelerating artificial intelligence by ensuring constant communication between systems. However, the complexity of healthcare systems makes it difficult to adopt these guidelines. Despite these constraints, compatibility enhances the efficiency and scalability of artificial intelligence, as demonstrated by successful applications in the healthcare field. It also acts as a driver for innovation and cooperation, with future trends promising further development for the potential of artificial intelligence in healthcare.

4.1.3 Data Management and Storage Solutions

An essential element in the successful use of artificial intelligence in healthcare is the creation and use of more efficient algorithms. To identify key details and help make decisions, algorithms need to examine a large amount of information. Machine learning and deep learning methods have performed well here, enabling patterns to be spotted and outcomes to be predicted more accurately. However, these methods require large amounts of computing power, which can be challenging for healthcare groups as they look to expand their use of artificial intelligence.

To meet computing needs, it is essential to take advantage of high-performance computing (HPC) and distributed computing frameworks. This technology enables large datasets to be processed in parallel, considerably reducing the time needed for model formation and inference. In addition, the use of edge computing can relieve the burden on central data centers by processing data closer to their source, reducing latency, and improving real-time decision-making capabilities in medical environments (Biswas & Singh, 2024). In addition to technological advances, the successful adoption of artificial intelligence in healthcare depends on the ability to develop a corporate culture that values innovation and change. Healthcare professionals need to be taught to collaborate with artificial intelligence systems to trust their results and recognize their limitations. Further education and professional development are needed to ensure that the workforce has the skills to use AI tools correctly (Harry, 2023).

In addition, regulatory and ethical issues need to be addressed to facilitate the proper expansion of artificial intelligence in healthcare. It is essential to comply with data protection regulations, such as HIPAA in the USA, to preserve patient confidentiality and trust. It is also necessary to define ethical criteria for the use of artificial intelligence, ensuring that algorithms are clear, explainable, and free from bias (Michel et al., 2024).

5.1 Case Studies of AI Scalability in Healthcare

5.1.1 Examples of Successful Implementation

As we examine the subtleties of artificial intelligence scalability in healthcare, it becomes clear that one of the key elements of its effectiveness is the ability to process and analyze large quantities of varied data. The complexity and diversity of medical data encompass everything from electronic health records to genetic information and real-time patient monitoring systems. The challenge is to put in place systems capable of efficiently integrating these data to provide comprehensive information while complying with strict security and confidentiality standards (Pasricha, 2023). Advanced data analytics and machine learning techniques have been used in scalable artificial intelligence solutions to address these challenges. For example, natural language processing (NLP) plays a key role in gathering valuable information from unstructured data, such as doctors' notes and medical literature, improving diagnostic accuracy, and adjusting treatment plans. Moreover, the integration of artificial intelligence into predictive analytics has revolutionized epidemic prediction and management, enabling rapid intervention and efficient resource allocation (Agafonov et al., 2024). The ability of artificial intelligence to adapt to different health environments, from small clinics to large hospital networks, is an important element. Cloud-based platforms enable adaptation by providing a flexible and scalable infrastructure, avoiding the need for large technology investments that are required in advance of healthcare providers. In addition, cloud solutions facilitate the continuous improvement of AI models by using global data to improve their accuracy and relevance. Interdisciplinary collaboration is crucial to ensure the effective growth of AI. Collaborations between data researchers, health professionals, and technology developers foster the emergence of innovative and practical artificial intelligence solutions. This collaboration has led to the development of AI tools that are both medically effective and compatible with caregiver workflows, reducing disruption and improving their usefulness.

The future of AI scalability in healthcare is expected to have significant transformative effects. With the progressive evolution of artificial intelligence models, progress in personalized medicine is anticipated, with a focus on treatments customized to each patient's specific genetic and daily life characteristics. Moreover, the flexibility of artificial intelligence is essential for improving accessibility to health by resolving disparities in disadvantaged areas through remote diagnostics and telemedicine solutions (Asan & Mansouri, 2023; Yu et al., 2023).

5.1.2 Lessons Identified from Failures

The growth of AI in health poses challenges that require a holistic approach that integrates technology, organizational dynamics, and human factors. Advances in cloud and edge computing play critical roles in facilitating scalable artificial intelligence solutions by providing essential computing power and storage capabilities. This technology simplifies the management of large datasets, which are crucial for building advanced AI models that generate reliable health outcomes (Strange, 2024).

Health institutions must foster a culture of innovation and continuous learning. This involves investing in digital literacy training for employees and creating an environment that is conducive to transition and adaptation. Leadership plays a crucial role in facilitating cultural change, preparing the workforce for the effective adoption of AI.

Human factors, such as ethical considerations and patient-centered care, play crucial roles in the application of artificial intelligence in healthcare. Ensuring transparency in AI decision-making processes, as well as prioritizing patient consent and data protection, is fundamental to fostering trust and accountability. By involving both patients and healthcare professionals in the development and implementation of AI solutions, we ensure that these technologies address real-world needs and enhance the quality of care. (Ness et al., 2024; Rajamäki et al., 2023). Strategic partnerships between technology companies, academic institutions, and health organizations can strengthen the growth capacity of AI in the health field. This collaboration leverages a variety of skills and resources, allowing for the exchange of knowledge and best practices. Alliances play a key role in solving scalability challenges by fostering standardization and interoperability between artificial intelligence systems. Improving artificial intelligence in healthcare requires a comprehensive strategy that takes into account technological, organizational, and human aspects. By taking a collaborative approach, healthcare stakeholders can harness the transformative potential of artificial intelligence, resulting in improved patient outcomes and a more efficient healthcare system. The search for scalable AI in health is complex; however, through careful planning and implementation, it has the potential to transform the industry (Agafonov et al., 2024; Pasricha, 2023; Sun & Zhou, 2023).

6.1 Future Directions for AI Scalability in Healthcare

6.1.1 Emerging Technologies

New technologies of artificial intelligence for health are transforming the framework for scalable solutions. Machine learning and deep learning play crucial roles in this evolution, enabling advanced data analysis and predictive modeling. Cloud computing can improve scalability by providing a robust infrastructure for the deployment of artificial intelligence. The evolution of natural language processing promotes interaction and data extraction in patients. Blockchain technology ensures secure data management, whereas IoT integration facilitates the connection of different health systems. Edge computing enables real-time data processing, while the arrival of 5G improves connectivity (Aljabri, 2022). Process automation increases operational efficiency, offering both challenges and opportunities in the implementation of these advanced technologies.

6.1.2 Policy and Regulation Development

Policies and regulatory frameworks are critical to the expansion of AI in health because they allow for a balance between promoting innovation and protecting patient safety and data privacy. Governments and regulatory bodies are essential to developing these policies; however, they face difficulties in developing universal regulations due to different health environments. Current regulations can hinder or encourage the implementation of AI, highlighting the importance of adaptive and flexible approaches (Palaniappan et al., 2024). It is essential to emphasize transparency and accountability in artificial intelligence systems, which requires collaboration among policymakers, technologists, and health professionals. Including ethical considerations and fostering international cooperation are essential for the global standardization of artificial intelligence policies (Ahuja, 2019; Beam & Kohane, 2018; Chen et al., 2019).

6.1.3 Potential Impact on Global Healthcare Systems

The agility of AI in health offers significant transformative potential for global systems. AI has the ability to improve patient outcomes by facilitating personalized treatment plans. Improved efficiency in the delivery of care and resource management leads to better diagnostic accuracy and earlier detection of diseases. Artificial intelligence has the ability to solve disparities in access to healthcare in disadvantaged areas while reducing costs through optimized procedures. This promotes international cooperation in medical research and provides health professionals with sophisticated decision-making tools (Zuhair et al., 2024). In addition, artificial intelligence has the ability to reduce staff shortages through the automation of routine tasks and accelerate the drug discovery process. Nevertheless, its extensive implementation raises potential ethical and confidentiality issues (Dyer, 2020; Evans, 2016).

7.1   Synthesis and Prospects for AI Scalability in Healthcare

The study of the scalability of artificial intelligence in the health sector reveals a complex terrain full of problems and potential. Understanding the complexities of AI scalability is crucial for effectively integrating AI into health systems. The challenges faced, such as data privacy issues, interoperability difficulties, and the need for resilient infrastructure, highlight the importance of strategic approaches to overcoming these barriers (Ghassemi et al., 2018). Technological advances offer promising solutions to these challenges. Advances in data management, cloud computing, and machine learning techniques play critical roles in improving the scalability of artificial intelligence systems. The cases studied highlight the tangible benefits of large-scale artificial intelligence, showcasing improvements in patient outcomes, operational efficiency, and decision-making processes. These cases illustrate healthcare institutions seeking to implement artificial intelligence on a large scale (Hinton & Salakhutdinov, 2006). The future of AI scalability in healthcare is promising. Continuous research and development, as well as multidisciplinary collaboration, will be critical to improving AI systems that are both scalable and ethical. It will be crucial to continue improving regulatory frameworks and implementing standardized procedures to facilitate this (Medicine, 2012).

8.1   Conclusion

To understand how artificial intelligence can potentially be extended into the health field, it is essential to consider the key elements that enable this transformation. The key to AI scalability is its ability to efficiently process and interpret large amounts of data and information. This is absolutely critical, as medical data are being generated and growing at an alarming rate through electronic medical records, medical imaging, and connected device technology. The application of this information when combined should increase the rate of accurate diagnosis, personalized treatment, and overall patient improvement. A major barrier to the adoption of AI on the healthcare scale is ensuring seamless data sharing and integration. Different healthcare providers and systems have different technology platforms and standards, resulting in gaps in data transfer and integration. Measures to be taken in this direction include the establishment of common protocols and the promotion of the use of interoperable systems. In addition, strengthening security regarding patient data and information is equally crucial. The more information that is shared, the more healthcare facilities are exposed to the risks of data dissemination and loss of confidence from their patients (Kees & Hargrove, 2021; Raghupathi & Raghupathi, 2014; Topol, 2019; Wirtz & Göttel, 2016).

Bibliography

Alandjani, G. (2023). Integrating AI with Green Internet of Things in Healthcare for Achieving UN's SDGs. *The Journal of Technology and Innovative Products in Technology*, 44(3), 513–521. https://doi.org/10.52783/tjjpt.v44.13.330

Agafonov, O., Babic, A., Sousa, S., & Alagaratnam, S. (2024). Editorial: Trustworthy AI for healthcare. *Frontiers in Digital Health*, 6. https://doi.org/10.3389/fdgth.2024.1427233

Ahuja, A. S. (2019). The Impact of Artificial Intelligence on Healthcare: A Systematic Review. *Journal of Healthcare Management*, 64(3), 151–166. https://doi.org/10.1097/JHM-D-18-00045

Aljabri, M. G. (2022). Blockchain Interoperability on Healthcare: A Systematic Review. *European Proceedings of Multidisciplinary Sciences*. https://doi.org/10.15405/epms.2022.10.58

Alsuliman, T., Humaidan, D., & Sliman, L. (2020). Machine learning and artificial intelligence in the service of medicine: Necessity or potentiality?. *Current Research in Translational Medicine*, 68(4), 245–251. https://doi.org/10.1016/j.retram.2020.01.002

Arigbabu, A. T., Olaniyi, O. O., Adigwe, C. S., Adebiyi, O. O., & Ajayi, S. A. (2024). Data Governance in AI - Enabled Healthcare Systems: A Case of the Project Nightingale. *Asian Journal of Research in Computer Science*, 17(5), 85–107. https://doi.org/10.9734/ajrcos/2024/v17i5441

Asan, O., & Mansouri, M. (2023). What May Impact Trustworthiness of AI in Digital Healthcare: Discussion from Patients' Viewpoint. *Proceedings of the International Symposium on Human Factors and Ergonomics in Health Care*, 12(1), 5–10. https://doi.org/10.1177/2327857923121001

Babarinde, A. O., Ayo-Farai, O., Maduka, C. P., Okongwu, C. C., Ogundairo, O., & Sodamade, O. T. (2023). Review of AI Applications in Healthcare: Comparative Insights from the USA and Africa. *International Medical Science Research Journal*, 3(3), 92–107. https://doi.org/10.51594/imsrj.v3i3.641.

Bajwa, J., Munir, U., Nori, A., & Williams, B. (2021). Artificial intelligence in healthcare: Transforming the practice of medicine. *Future Healthcare Journal*, 8(2), e188–e194. https://doi.org/10.7861/fhj.2021-0095

Banerjee, A., & Kumar, S. (2024). Artificial Intelligence in Healthcare. In *Green Industrial Applications of Artificial Intelligence and Internet of Things* (pp. 46–60). Bentham Science Publishers.

Beam, A. L., & Kohane, I. S. (2018). Big Data and Machine Learning in Health Care. *Journal of the American Medical Association*, 319(13), 1317–1318. https://doi.org/10.1001/jama.2018.0048

Bhagat, I. A., et al. (2024). Artificial Intelligence in Healthcare: A Review. *International Journal of Scientific Research in Science, Engineering, and Technology*, 11(4), 133-138.

Biswas, M. I., & Singh, D. R. K. (2024). "Application of AI and Blockchain in Healthcare Industry" – A Review. *Journal of Advanced Zoology*. https://doi.org/10.53555/jaz.v45i2.3983

Chauhan, A., et al. (2024). AI in Healthcare. *International Journal of Advanced Research in Science, Communication and Technology*, 623–628. https://doi.org/10.48175/ijarsct-18692

Chen, M., Ma, Y., Li, Y., Wu, D., & Zhang, Y. (2019). Wearable 2.0: Enabling Human and Ambient Sensing for Pervasive Healthcare. *IEEE Internet of Things Journal*, 6(2), 2919–2929. https://doi.org/10.1109/JIOT.2018.2888838

Chidi, N. R., & Odimba, N. U. (2024). AI Applications in Screening and Diagnosis of Diabetic Retinopathy in Rural Settings. *International Medical Science Research Journal*, 4(3), 266–275. https://doi.org/10.51594/imsrj.v4i3.918

Chowdhury, R. H. (2024). Intelligent Systems for Healthcare Diagnostics and Treatment. *World Journal of Advanced Research and Reviews*, 23(1), 7–15.

Cohen, R. Y., & Kovacheva, V. P. (2023). A Methodology for a Scalable, Collaborative, and Resource-Efficient Platform, MERLIN, to Facilitate Healthcare AI Research. *IEEE Journal of Biomedical and Health Informatics*, 27(6), 3014–3025.

Dhawan, S., & Kumar, K. (2024). Ethical Implications of AI in Healthcare. *Indian Scientific Journal of Research in Engineering and Management*, 8(3), 1–13. https://doi.org/10.55041/ijsrem29006

Dyer, O. (2020). Health AI: Privacy Concerns Loom as Regulators Catch Up with Technology. *British Medical Journal*, 371, m4765. https://doi.org/10.1136/bmj.m4765

Esmaeilzadeh, P. (2024). Challenges and Strategies for Wide-Scale Artificial Intelligence (AI) Deployment in Healthcare Practices: A Perspective for Healthcare Organizations. *Artificial Intelligence in Medicine*, 151, 102861.

Ethical Considerations in AI-Enabled Big Data Research: Balancing Innovation and Privacy. (2020). https://doi.org/10.52783/ijca.v13i03.38350

Evans, R. S. (2016). Electronic Health Records: Then, Now, and in the Future. *Journal of Healthcare Information Management*, 30(1), 4–10.

Ghassemi, M., Naumann, T., & Denecke, K. (2018). A Systematic Review of the Machine Learning Algorithms for Health Monitoring. *Artificial Intelligence in Medicine*, 86, 109–125. https://doi.org/10.1016/j.artmed.2018.05.011

Gopi, B., Kokila, M. S., Bibin, C. V., Sasikala, D., Howard, E., & Boopathi, S. (2024). Distributed Technologies Using AI/ML Techniques for Healthcare Applications. In *Social Innovations in Education, Environment, and Healthcare* (pp. 375–396). IGI Global.

Haleem, A., Javaid, M., Singh, R. P., Suman, R., & Rab, S. (2021). Blockchain technology applications in healthcare: An overview. *International Journal of Intelligent Networks*, 2, 130-139. https://doi.org/10.1016/j.ijin.2021.09.005

Harry, A. (2023). The Future of Medicine: Harnessing the Power of AI for Revolutionizing Healthcare. *International Journal of Multidisciplinary Sciences and Arts*, 2(1), 36–47. https://doi.org/10.47709/ijmdsa.v2i1.2395

Hinton, G., & Salakhutdinov, R. (2006). Reducing the Dimensionality of Data with Neural Networks. *Science*, 313(5786), 504–507. https://doi.org/10.1126/science.1127647

Hoseini, M. (2023). Patient Experiences with AI in Healthcare Settings. *AI and Tech in Behavioral and Social Sciences*, 1(3), 12–18. https://doi.org/10.61838/kman.aitech.1.3.3

Institute of Medicine. (2012). *Best Care at Lower Cost: The Path to Continuously Learning Health Care in America*. National Academies Press. https://doi.org/10.17226/13444

Kees, A., & Hargrove, R. (2021). The Future of Artificial Intelligence in Healthcare: The Role of Regulatory Frameworks. *Health Informatics Journal*, 27(1), 146–158. https://doi.org/10.1177/1460458220940245

Kesan, J., & Shah, R. (2008). Open Standards in Electronic Governance. *Proceedings of the 2nd International Conference on Theory and Practice of Electronic Governance*, 75, 179–182. https://doi.org/10.1145/1509096.1509132

Kolasa, K., Admassu, B., Hołownia-Voloskova, M., Kędzior, K. J., Poirrier, J. E., & Perni, S. (2023). Systematic reviews of machine learning in healthcare: a literature review. *Expert Review of Pharmacoeconomics & Outcomes Research*, 24(1), 63–115. https://doi.org/10.1080/14737167.2023.2279107

McClintock, D. S. (2024, April). Clinical AI Model Translation and Deployment: Creating a Scalable, Standardized, and Responsible AI Lifecycle Framework in Healthcare. In *Medical Imaging 2024: Digital and Computational Pathology* (Vol. 12933, p. 129330G). SPIE.

Michel, L. H., Reis, A. A., Cornet, A. D., Jacobien, H. F., Oosterhoff, J. H., Townsend, R., Bommel, J., & Gommers, D. (2024). Charting a New Course in Healthcare: Early-Stage AI Algorithm Registration to Enhance Trust And Transparency. *NPJ Digital Medicine*, 7(1). https://doi.org/10.1038/s41746-024-01104-w

Mishra, I., Kashyap, V., Pahwa, R., & Dheivanai, R. (2024). Revolutionizing Healthcare: The Impact and Growth of Artificial Intelligence (AI). *International Research Journal on Advanced Engineering Hub (IRJAEH)*, 2(7), 1875–1881.

Nahavandi, D., Alizadehsani, R., Khosravi, A., & Acharya, U. R. (2022). Application of artificial intelligence in wearable devices: Opportunities and challenges. *Computer Methods and Programs in Biomedicine*, 213, Article 106541. https://doi.org/10.1016/j.cmpb.2021.106541

Naik, N., et al. (2022). Legal and Ethical Consideration in Artificial Intelligence in Healthcare: Who Takes Responsibility? Front Surg, 9:862322. doi: 10.3389/fsurg.2022.862322.

Ness, S., Xuan, T. R., & Oguntibeju, O. O. (2024). Influence of AI: Robotics in Healthcare. *Asian Journal of Research in Computer Science*, 17(5), 222–237. https://doi.org/10.9734/ajrcos/2024/v17i5451

Palaniappan, K., Yan, E., & Vogel, S. (2024). Global Regulatory Frameworks for the Use of Artificial Intelligence (AI) in the Healthcare Services Sector. *Healthcare*, 12(5), 562–562. https://doi.org/10.3390/healthcare12050562

Panayides, A. S., Amini, A., Filipovic, N. D., Sharma, A., Tsaftaris, S. A., Young, A., Foran, D., Do, N., Golemati, S., Kurc, T., Huang, K., Nikita, K. S., Veasey, B. P., Zervakis, M., Saltz, J. H., & Pattichis, C. S. (2020). AI in medical imaging informatics: Current challenges and future directions. *IEEE Journal of Biomedical and Health Informatics*, 24(7), 1837–1857. https://doi.org/10.1109/JBHI.2020.2991043

Pasricha, S. (2023). AI Ethics in Smart Healthcare. *IEEE Consumer Electronics Magazine*, 12(4), 12–20. https://doi.org/10.1109/mce.2022.3220001

Peixoto, H., Domingues, A., & Fernandes, B. (2016). Steps toward Interoperability in Healthcare Environment. *Applying Business Intelligence to Clinical and Healthcare Organizations*, 1–23. https://doi.org/10.4018/978-1-4666-9882-6.ch001

Raghupathi, W., & Raghupathi, V. (2014). Big Data Analytics in Healthcare: Promise and Potential. *Health Information Science and Systems*, 2(1), 1–10. https://doi.org/10.1186/s13755-014-0002-2

Rajamäki, J., Gioulekas, F., Rocha, P., Garcia, X., Ofem, P., & Tyni, J. (2023). ALTAI Tool for Assessing AI-Based Technologies: Lessons Learned and Recommendations from SHAPES Pilots. *Healthcare*, 11(10), 1454. https://doi.org/10.3390/healthcare11101454

Rich, E., et al. (2024). AI in Healthcare. *International Journal of Advanced Research in Science, Communication and Technology*.

Roppelt, J. S., Kanbach, D. K., & Kraus, S. (2024). Artificial intelligence in healthcare institutions: A systematic literature review on influencing factors. *Technology in Society*, 76, 102443. https://doi.org/10.1016/j.techsoc.2023.102443.

Schork, N. J. (2019). Artificial intelligence and personalized medicine. *Cancer Treatment and Research*, 178, 265–283. https://doi.org/10.1007/978-3-030-16391-4_11

Sharma, A. (2024). Artificial Intelligence in Healthcare. In *Revolutionizing the Healthcare Sector with AI* (pp. 1–25). IGI Global.

Shende, A. (2022). Integrating AI and Distributed Computing for Advanced Dental Healthcare Management. *Journal of Artificial Intelligence & Cloud Computing*, 1–3. https://doi.org/10.47363/jaicc/2022(1)239

Singh, K. D., & Singh, P. (2024). Fog Cloud Computing and IoT Integration for AI enabled Autonomous Systems in Robotics. *EAI Endorsed Transactions on AI and Robotics*, 3. https://doi.org/10.4108/airo.3617

Strange, M. (2024). Three Different Types of AI Hype in Healthcare. *AI and Ethics*, 4(3), 833–840. https://doi.org/10.1007/s43681-024-00465-y

Sun, G., & Zhou, Y. (2023). AI in Healthcare: Navigating Opportunities and Challenges in Digital Communication. *Frontiers in Digital Health*, 5. https://doi.org/10.3389/fdgth.2023.1291132

Talati, D. (2023). AI in Healthcare Domain. *Journal of Knowledge Learning and Science Technology* (Online), 2(3), 256–262.

Tilala, M. H., Chenchala, P. K., Choppadandi, A., Kaur, J., Naguri, S., Saoji, R., & Devaguptapu, B. (2024). Ethical considerations in the use of artificial intelligence and machine learning in health care: A comprehensive review. *Cureus*, 16(6), e61522. https://doi.org/10.7759/cureus.61522

Topol, E. J. (2019). *Deep Medicine: How Artificial Intelligence Can Make Healthcare Human Again*. Basic Books.

Tothy, A. S., Sastry, S. K., Valencia, A., Springman, M. K., & Murphy, S. (2016). Showcasing Patient Experience and Engagement Best Practices through an Innovative Forum Celebrating Patients, Families, and Multidisciplinary Care Teams. *Patient Experience Journal*, 3(2), 83–86. https://doi.org/10.35680/2372-0247.1127

Wang, J. K., Ding, J., & Niu, T. (2012). *Interoperability and Standardization of Intercloud Cloud Computing*. ArXiv (Cornell University). https://doi.org/10.48550/arxiv.1212.5956

White, S. E. (2014). A review of big data in health care: Challenges and opportunities. Open Access *Bioinformatics*, 6, 13–18.

Wirtz, B. W., & Göttel, V. (2016). Business Model Innovation: Opportunities and Challenges for Hospitals. *Journal of Health Management*, 18(2), 233–248. https://doi.org/10.1177/0972063416632901

Yu, K. H., Beam, A. L., & Kohane, I. S. (2018). Artificial intelligence in healthcare. *Nature Biomedical Engineering*, 2(10), 719–731. https://doi.org/10.1038/s41551-018-0305-z

Yu, P., Xu, H., Hu, X., & Deng, C. (2023). Leveraging Generative AI and Large Language Models: A Comprehensive Roadmap for Healthcare Integration. *Healthcare*, 11(20), 2776. https://doi.org/10.3390/healthcare11202776

Zahlan, A., Ranjan, R. P., & Hayes, D. (2023). Artificial intelligence innovation in healthcare: Literature review, exploratory analysis, and future research. *Technology in Society*, 74, 102321. https://doi.org/10.1016/j.techsoc.2023.102321

Zuhair, V., Babar, A., Ali, R., Oduoye, M. O., Noor, Z., Chris, K., Okon, I. I., & Rehman, L. U. (2024). Exploring the impact of artificial intelligence on global health and enhancing healthcare in developing nations. *Journal of Primary Care & Community Health*, 15, 21501319241245847. https://doi.org/10.1177/21501319241245847

2 Fundamental Principles of AI Scalability in Healthcare

Abdallah Ahmed Wajdi, Houneida Sakly, Ramzi Guetari, and Naoufel Kraiem

2.1 Introduction

2.1.1 Overview of AI in Healthcare

The transformation of the health sector is underway through the integration of artificial intelligence (AI), which faces many challenges, such as rising prices, limited access, and the need for personalized care. The impact of artificial intelligence extends to various areas, such as improving medical decision-making, simplifying hospital operations, improving medical image analysis, and advancing patient management through portable artificial intelligence devices. The potential applications of AI in healthcare are very wide. Innovative technologies such as artificial intelligence-based sensory devices enable continuous patient monitoring, while virtual nursing assistants provide ongoing support. Telemedicine facilitates advanced diagnostics and consultations, improving efficiency and empowering patients to take control of their health. Complementing these advancements, Natural Language Processing (NLP) plays a crucial role in accelerating healthcare AI by efficiently processing clinical data. The Mayo Clinic's NLP-as-a-service implementation exemplifies how scalable and resource-efficient NLP solutions can revolutionize healthcare delivery (Wen et al., 2019).

However, the use of artificial intelligence in healthcare also poses challenges, such as concerns about data confidentiality, algorithmic biases, and the requirement for model accuracy and reliability. To overcome these challenges, it is essential to consider the issues that are central to healthcare practices and foster a cultural evolution that sees artificial intelligence as an advantage rather than a threat. As the global adoption of AI in the healthcare field increases, it is essential to prioritize ethical considerations around data protection, consent, and stigma. Ensuring the responsible and ethical use of AI technologies, as well as efforts to promote equitable and affordable access, will create a more effective, data-driven, and patient-centered healthcare system.

The future of healthcare is promising, with artificial intelligence poised to play a critical role in personalizing medicine, discovering new drugs, and solving global health challenges. Collaboration among technology developers, healthcare providers, policymakers, and patients will be critical to harnessing

DOI: 10.1201/9781003480594-2

Table 2.1 AI-powered technologies for patient care and monitoring

Main applications	Key technologies and applications	Benefits	Challenges
AI-powered wearable devices	Continuous physiological monitoring (heart rate, blood pressure, etc.); early detection of health issues; personalized recommendations for lifestyle changes	Improved patient engagement; proactive health management	Data collection and model deployment; balancing accuracy with wearable device limitations
Virtual nursing assistants	24/7 patient support and health reminders; chronic disease management; patient education and behavior monitoring	Enhanced patient engagement and education; improved treatment plan compliance	Data privacy and information accuracy; ensuring they complement human care
AI in telemedicine and remote patient engagement	Advanced diagnostics and consultations; personalized virtual consultations; remote patient monitoring and predictive analytics	Increased healthcare accessibility; proactive chronic condition care	Data privacy, system accuracy, and integration

Source: Reference (Varnosfaderani & Forouzanfar, 2024)

the transformative potential of artificial intelligence to foster a healthcare environment that is ethically driven and patient-centered, as described in Table 2.1. (See reference: (Varnosfaderani & Forouzanfar, 2024).

2.1.2   *Importance of Scalability in Healthcare AI*

Expanding the use of artificial intelligence (AI) in healthcare is crucial to transforming patient management and care delivery. As healthcare institutions increasingly adopt AI solutions, developing this technology and customizing it for specific needs become essential. The integration of AI tools poses challenges, such as managing various medical data and moving AI models from prototypes to real clinical applications (Cohen et al., 2023).

Ensuring the scalability of artificial intelligence in healthcare is essential. Companies must develop artificial intelligence systems capable of managing growing volumes of data, adapting to changing medical needs, and maintaining performance despite varying workloads. Strong infrastructure, optimization techniques, and cloud solutions are needed to meet the growing demands of AI applications.

Another key consideration is the safe and ethical use of artificial intelligence in healthcare. Clear rules are essential for building trust and guiding ethical practices. This will address transparency, model accuracy, data quality control, accountability, and ethical issues. Through investment in financial resources and human capital development, continuous learning initiatives, and the creation of an enabling environment for AI integration, health organizations can better address the challenges of AI growth. Successful case studies highlight how large-scale AI systems have been effectively implemented in medical environments to improve patient outcomes, enhance operational efficiency, and foster innovation in different medical specialties. The lessons learned from past experiences and emerging technologies that impact scalability suggest a future where personalized patient experiences, early detection capabilities, enhanced clinical skills, and improved operational efficiency are no longer just goals but achievable realities.

In summary, scalability in medical artificial intelligence is paramount. It is crucial to adopt effective growth strategies to harness the transformative potential of artificial intelligence while responsibly addressing associated risks. By taking a step back and adopting new approaches to address scalability challenges such as data management, model deployment, infrastructure needs, operational efficiency, regulatory compliance, and quality assurance, healthcare actors such as doctors, nurses, and patients can discover great benefits. See references: (Esmaeilzadeh, 2024), (Spatharou et al., 2020), (Vultr Industry Cloud Solutions – Healthcare and Life Sciences – Vultr, 2024), and (Healthcare Triangle, 2024).

2.2   Challenges of Scaling Data in Healthcare AI

2.2.1   Managing Large and Diverse Healthcare Data

Managing healthcare data is critical to advancing AI systems in the healthcare field. The integration of various types of data, such as electronic healthcare records (EHR), genetics, and real-time device information, presents both challenges and opportunities. A major challenge is the lack of standardized data formats and technical interoperability, which limits the possibilities for large-scale applications of big data and artificial intelligence. The use of standardized formats such as fast healthcare interoperability resources can facilitate data harmonization, allowing raw hospital records to be converted into AI-compatible formats (Dash et al., 2019).

Data harmonization pipelines (DHPs), such as the FHIR-DHP, are essential for effectively managing large amounts of clinical data. These pipelines simplify the process by extracting data from hospital databases, aligning it with FHIR standards, validating the syntax and converting it into patient models before exporting it in formats suitable for artificial intelligence applications. To foster collaboration between stakeholders, improve interoperability, and improve the quality of patient care through customized data design, DHPs play a key role in healthcare. The automation of clinical data acquisition further enhances the scalability of artificial intelligence by easily integrating different data sources. Managing large amounts of medical data is essential for creating robust AI models that can adapt to different patient demands. By implementing scalable platforms such as FHIR-DHPs and

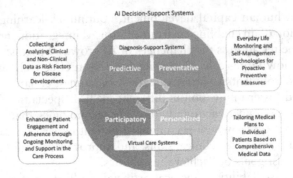

Figure 2.1 Categories and features of AI decision-support systems.

maintaining security standards while using cloud solutions such as CaDP, healthcare organizations can improve their operational efficiency and drive innovation.

In summary, the effective management of a wide range of medical data through simplified harmonization pipelines is essential to ensure the efficient growth of AI systems in health. By solving problems such as nonstandardized formats, gaps in technical interoperability, and limited collaboration between actors, organizations can fully exploit the potential of big data and artificial intelligence, ultimately transforming healthcare management as seen in Figure 2.1. See references: (AI Scalability In Healthcare Workload Scaling, 2024), (AI Scalability in Health Solutions, 2024), and (Williams et al., 2023).

2.2.2 Data Security and Privacy Concerns

Ensuring data security and confidentiality is crucial to ensure the growth of artificial intelligence in health. The confidential nature of medical data, such as medical records and treatment plans, requires stringent security measures to prevent unauthorized access and data breaches. Ensuring data quality is essential to ensure the proper functioning of AI systems and to avoid erroneous models and decisions. The data management framework should establish standardized collection procedures, advanced cleaning techniques, and rigorous access controls to preserve patient information. Compliance with regulations such as HIPAA is essential for maintaining security and privacy standards in the industry. Engaging with regulatory bodies can strengthen these efforts by following guidelines such as the EU's Ethics for Reliable Artificial Intelligence or the Biden administration's model for a rights law of AI. By implementing robust security measures such as encryption, access limitations, multifactor authentication, threat detection tools, and regular security audits, healthcare companies can reduce the risk of data breaches. With the rise of cloud computing and automation in medical data management, it is essential to focus on security protocols to preserve patient information.

Automation can optimize tasks such as data entry and reporting while maintaining stringent security standards. In addition, the integration of advanced technologies such as blockchain provides a decentralized and transparent platform for securely storing and managing healthcare data. In short, ensuring data security and confidentiality in the field of medical artificial intelligence is crucial to protecting patient information from unauthorized access and guaranteeing compliance with regulations. Through the adoption of strong security measures, collaboration with regulatory authorities, and the use of innovative technologies such as blockchain, health organizations can effectively protect their sensitive data during this era of digital transformation. See references: (Kasyapa & Vanmathi, 2024), (Staff, 2024), and (AI Implementation in Healthcare: 10 Challenges and Solutions, 2024).

2.3 Challenges of Scaling Models in Healthcare AI

2.3.1 *Transitioning AI Models from Prototypes to Clinical Deployment*

The transition from prototype AI models to clinical applications represents a major advance in healthcare. Despite the integration of artificial intelligence, careful consideration of the challenges related to scalability and reliability is essential. One major challenge is the efficient management of different data streams, which requires fundamental models such as MedImageInsight. This approach allows one to manage large image integrations without requiring site-specific training, thereby improving scalability. In addition, by integrating uncertainty limits, artificial intelligence systems can adapt to variations in dynamic clinical environments.

The verification of AI models via real data from prestigious institutions such as the Massachusetts General Hospital highlights the importance of recognizing large changes in data and their impact on the performance of the model. The MMC+ model acts as an early warning system to identify potential performance declines, emphasizing the importance of continuous monitoring and rapid interventions to maintain the reliability of the model.

MMC+ highlights significant advances in the management of various data streams and the ability to be scalable, offering a solid and affordable solution suitable for real medical applications. By focusing on the integration of case-based artificial intelligence solutions into everyday practice, this framework paves the way for more advanced decision-support tools. These advances foster a culture that accepts artificial intelligence as an essential part of the health ecosystem. In summary, to successfully transition from AI models to medical environments, addressing the challenges of managing various data, ensuring scalability, and maintaining model reliability is necessary. Using advances such as uncertainty limits and fundamental models, health organizations can overcome these barriers, revealing the transformative impact of artificial intelligence on patient management. See references: (Merkow et al., 2024) and (Spatharou et al., 2020).

2.3.2   *Ensuring Model Accuracy and Reliability*

Ensuring the accuracy and reliability of AI models to expand systems in the healthcare sector presents a major challenge in reconciling statistical bias and variance. Complex models may be too well-suited to observations, whereas simpler models may lack key reasons. This compensation highlights the importance of optimization methods in determining the appropriate level of predictive accuracy. It is crucial for prediction and disease models to assess performance indicators at the individual scale and identify influencing variables in a comprehensible way.

It is essential to maintain security and confidence in AI models by explaining their decision-making processes. In the field of medical AI, the use of different recurrent neural network (RNN) models allows for an autonomous evaluation of data provided at different stages, which improves predictability and reliability. The objective of these advances is to bridge the gap between model accuracy and explainability, which is critical for clinical relevance and patient safety. In addition, the use of association rule mining based on biological relationships between data elements can improve the clarity of artificial intelligence models used for complex health datasets. Future AI models should focus on transparency to build trust in medical environments. Using innovative methods such as visualization and functional validation of results, it is possible to maintain high accuracy and reliability in medical artificial intelligence systems. In addition, ongoing research should focus on improving the interpretability of the model, particularly in situations where biological links are not fully understood, such as complex imaging analyses or linguistic data analysis.

In summary, the development of artificial intelligence in the healthcare field should focus on improving model accuracy and reliability through a combination of optimization strategies, explainable artificial intelligence principles, and innovative validation techniques. See references: (Mennella et al., 2024), (Varnosfaderani & Forouzanfar, 2024), and (Lee et al., 2021).

2.4   Challenges of Scaling Infrastructure in Healthcare AI

2.4.1   *Robust Infrastructure Requirements*

To effectively expand AI systems in the healthcare field, it is crucial to address key elements such as data retention, processing capabilities, and network efficiency. We need modern networks to ensure the fast and secure transfer of medical data needed for AI algorithms, as legacy networks with limited capacity and frequent outages do not meet these requirements.

Cloud computing, such as Google Cloud, offers scalable solutions to securely store and process large amounts of medical data. Using cloud-based machine learning tools such as BigQuery and Vertex AI, healthcare organizations can quickly analyze data, making it easier to make informed decisions about patient care. The cloud provides the flexibility and computing power to manage complex AI algorithms efficiently (Tawalbeh & Habeeb, 2018).

Investing in infrastructure elements such as GPU servers, data warehouses and development platforms are essential for laying the foundation for artificial intelligence systems in the healthcare sector. It is also important that organizations prioritize the hiring of specialized personnel, such as AI engineers, to ensure the successful implementation and development of artificial intelligence models. GPT-in-a-Box from vendors such as Nutanix can facilitate the establishment of an artificial intelligence infrastructure, allowing institutions to focus on creating models rather than addressing physical challenges. Modern networks increase the capacity for growth, allowing healthcare organizations to manage an increasing number of AI activities without compromising quality performance. In addition, advanced encryption and cybersecurity measures protect sensitive patient data from potential breaches, ensuring confidentiality and reliability. Network modernization also enables seamless integration into the cloud, which facilitates storage flexibility and access to data across different environments.

By consequence, building a strong infrastructure to expand AI systems in the healthcare sector requires the use of advanced networks, cloud computing solutions, and specialized hardware as described in Figure 2.2. By effectively addressing these issues, healthcare organizations can improve the efficiency and reliability of their AI implementations while maintaining safety standards and regulatory compliance. See references: (AI Scalability In Healthcare Workload Scaling, 2024), (Cloud Computing in Healthcare: Top 9 Benefits Revealed | Symphony Solutions, 2024), (Chinthakunta, 2024), and (Tawalbeh & Habeeb, 2018).

2.4.2 Implementing Cloud Solutions for Scalability

The cloud is critical for addressing the scalability challenges faced by AI systems in healthcare. Using a cloud infrastructure, such as Vultr's flexible

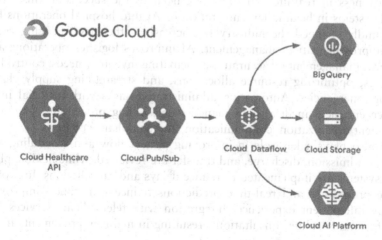

Figure 2.2 Cloud Healthcare API data workflow.

solutions and the robust Google Cloud platform, provides healthcare organizations with the flexibility and adaptability needed for effective growth.

Vultr's Cloud GPU, powered by AMD and NVIDIA accelerators, delivers scalable artificial intelligence solutions to regulatory-compliant healthcare organizations while facilitating personalized, genetic, and diagnostic support. In addition, Vultr's multicloud and edge solutions enable vendors to efficiently manage high-performance computing tasks such as genetic sequencing and medical imaging. In contrast, the Google Cloud Healthcare platform plays a critical role in healthcare innovation by securing patient data retention and providing access to advanced analytics and artificial intelligence/machine learning tools for developing advanced healthcare services. However, despite the benefits of using Google Cloud in the healthcare field, it is essential to carefully consider challenges such as data privacy issues and regulatory compliance to ensure successful implementation.

Vultr and Google Cloud show how cloud solutions can meet infrastructure requirements to extend AI systems in the healthcare industry. Using cloud computing technologies, healthcare organizations can improve data management, ensure data security and protection, and improve operational efficiency in real-world applications. In short, the integration of cloud solutions for scalability is essential to overcome the challenges faced by AI systems in the healthcare sector. By selecting the right cloud infrastructure provider, such as Vultr or Google Cloud, companies can effectively scale their AI operations while maintaining security, safety, and regulatory compliance. See references: (Vultr Industry Cloud Solutions – Healthcare and Life Sciences – Vultr, 2024) and (Broshkov, 2024).

2.5 Challenges of Scaling Operations in Healthcare AI

2.5.1 *Operational Efficiency in Real-world Settings*

Effectiveness in real-life situations is crucial to the successful integration of AI systems in health. The integration of AI into hospital operations has profoundly changed the industry by increasing efficiency, reducing costs, and improving patient management. AI improves logistics operations and resource management by accurately anticipating inventory needs, controlling facilities, optimizing resource allocations, and streamlining supply chains during emergencies. Automating administrative tasks with artificial intelligence enhances medical data management, billing procedures, planning, document organization, communication, and compliance control.

AI also plays a key role in improving patient flow and scheduling efficiency. Admission, discharge, and transfer are reviewed, while flexible planning systems are implemented to reduce delays and cancellations. Improved triage procedures and real-time predictions reduce wait times, improving the overall patient experience. Integration with telemedicine services further facilitates online consultations, resulting in major improvements in the operational efficiency of healthcare businesses. The implementation of scalable and customized artificial intelligence models adapted to different specialties and mixed payments offers many benefits in the field of healthcare management. Adopting cloud-based artificial intelligence systems allows for easy expansion and integrates adaptive learning algorithms that improve performance over time. This approach has led to a decrease in the number of claims rejected and improvements in payment days. In particular, the successful expansion of three to five hospitals without major infrastructure changes illustrates how scalable artificial intelligence solutions can have positive results in healthcare settings.

Operational efficiency is critical to the effective use of AI systems in healthcare. By optimizing logistics and resource management, automating administrative functions, and improving patient flow and planning through AI-based solutions, caregivers can significantly improve their overall outcomes while ensuring smooth transitions during periods of growth, as depicted in Table 2.2 through various aspects of AI application in IT healthcare systems. See references: (AI Scalability in Healthcare Workload Scaling, 2024), (Varnosfaderani & Forouzanfar, 2024), and (Barr, 2024).

Table 2.2 Transformative applications of AI in hospital management

Aspect	Applications
AI for hospital logistics and resource management	Predictive inventory management for medical supplies, pharmaceuticals, and equipment; efficient facilities management encompassing HVAC systems and predictive maintenance; optimization of resource allocation for personnel and commodities; and optimization and management of supply chains during emergencies and health crises.
Automating administrative tasks with AI	Management of patient data encompassing electronic medical records and analysis of unstructured data; automation of billing and claims processing to ensure accuracy and compliance; AI-enhanced scheduling systems for appointments and procedures; automation of document management and processing; automated communication and reminders to enhance patient engagement; and monitoring of data security and compliance.
AI in patient flow and scheduling optimization	Enhancement of patient flow via predictive analysis of admissions, discharges, and transfers; implementation of dynamic scheduling systems for appointments and procedures to reduce no-shows and cancellations; minimization of waiting times through improved triage processes and real-time patient wait time forecasting; and augmentation of patient experience by delivering precise information and integrating telehealth services for virtual consultations.

Source: Reference (Varnosfaderani & Forouzanfar, 2024)

2.5.2 *Regulatory Compliance and Quality Assurance*

It is critical to maintain regular standards and quality control when expanding AI systems in the healthcare sector. As these systems evolve to handle large amounts of sensitive data, ensuring compliance with strict regulations becomes increasingly difficult. The integration of artificial intelligence into healthcare operations poses serious challenges in terms of regulatory compliance, given the variety of standards and guidelines across different geographic regions. In the US, for example, the FDA is actively working to establish clear guidelines for artificial intelligence-based medical devices, making it even more difficult to comply with ever-changing regulations. The approval process for AI-based systems can be lengthy and complex, requiring rigorous evaluation and validation to meet legal requirements. It is crucial to demonstrate the safety and effectiveness of AI models while upholding ethical principles, especially when regulatory authorities focus on issues related to confidentiality, bias, and transparency. Compliance with data protection laws such as GDPR and HIPAA is another major hurdle, requiring strong measures to protect patient data. To effectively manage this complex regulatory environment, a proactive approach is essential. Creating transparent regulatory frameworks that foster trust, ensure safety, and guide the ethical application of AI in healthcare is essential. It is crucial to constantly monitor performance to ensure continued compliance with laws and regulations throughout the life of an AI system. By focusing on regulatory compliance and quality assurance, healthcare institutions can overcome the challenges of scalability while preserving patient well-being and confidentiality. See references: (Varnosfaderani & Forouzanfar, 2024) and (sdettech, 2024).

2.6 Strategies for Efficient Scaling of AI Systems in Healthcare

2.6.1 *Optimization Techniques for Scaleability*

To improve the scalability of AI systems in the healthcare sector, a holistic approach is essential. Using performance profiling tools such as TensorFlow Profiler, PyTorch Profiler, and NVIDIA Nsight can help pinpoint IT bottlenecks and resource usage patterns for precise optimization. In addition, methods such as quantization, pruning, and knowledge distillation for model optimization can reduce the complexity and size of models, which improves inference speed and reduces resource requirements for effective deployment. GPUs, TPUs, and FPGAs can significantly improve the performance of AI tasks. Cloud service providers offer specialized instances that support these accelerators to further improve their scalability.

Implementing these different strategies can significantly improve operational efficiency in healthcare settings. With these methods, artificial intelligence models are equipped to effectively manage the complexities of task growth by improving both their performance and accuracy. By using advanced tools and optimization techniques, healthcare institutions can simplify their procedures, respond effectively to demands, and provide fast insights powered by artificial intelligence to achieve superior patient outcomes. Finally, it is crucial to focus on optimization methods such as profiling tools, model optimization methods, and computer acceleration to address the challenges of growing AI systems in healthcare. This approach allows for more efficient implementation of AI models in medical environments, which will improve operational efficiency and ensure good patient management. See references: (AI Scalability in Healthcare Workload Scaling, 2024) and (Varnosfaderani & Forouzanfar, 2024).

2.6.2 Ensuring the Safety and Ethical Use of AI

Ensuring safety and ethical standards in the use of AI in healthcare is essential due to the challenges of transparency and explanation. Healthcare professionals need to understand the rationale behind artificial intelligence recommendations so that they can be confident, which is essential for patient well-being. A promising approach to address this issue is explainable AI (XAI), which illuminates decision-making processes of artificial intelligence models, thus enabling better understanding and trust between healthcare providers and patients. It is also crucial to obtain the approval of stakeholders to integrate artificial intelligence effectively into healthcare practices. Patients are often concerned about the reliability and implications of AI decisions, whereas clinicians may be worried about losing control or questioning the accuracy of these recommendations. To address these concerns, comprehensive training programs and collaborative environments are essential, enabling healthcare professionals to effectively use and validate AI tools, which promotes trust and acceptance. Another essential element of the ethical use of artificial intelligence in healthcare is data confidentiality. Federated learning offers a feasible solution by allowing algorithms to learn from local data stored within different healthcare entities without having to share sensitive information directly. This approach enhances data protection and security while maintaining patient privacy, which is essential in a sector where data protection is paramount. By focusing on transparency through artificial intelligence, involving relevant stakeholders to build trust, and implementing secure solutions such as shared learning for data protection, it is possible to achieve the ethical adoption of artificial intelligence in health. These approaches address key issues related to involvement, preserving clinician autonomy, and verifying accuracy and privacy, opening the way for responsible integration of scalable artificial intelligence systems in medical settings. See references: (Varnosfaderani & Forouzanfar, 2024) and (Liu et al., 2021).

2.7 Case Studies on the Successful Implementation of Scaled AI Systems in Healthcare

2.7.1 Examples of AI Deployment in Clinical Settings

An exemplary illustration of the use of artificial intelligence in medical environments can be seen in the success of a modular, cloud-based AI system used for revenue cycle management. This system was designed to meet different specialties and different types of payments, highlighting the flexibility and expansion of artificial intelligence in the healthcare field. Through the use of adaptive learning algorithms, AI models continue to improve their performance, resulting in a 25% decrease in credit denials and a 15% increase in credit cashing days. Interestingly, this adaptive AI system has been able to expand from three hospitals to five hospitals without major infrastructure changes. This overview illustrates how scalable and customizable AI solutions can lead to important improvements in health administration, resulting in increased operational efficiency and financial results. See reference: (Barr, 2024).

2.7.2   *Lessons Learned from Previous Implementation*

Past experiences with artificial intelligence in the healthcare field reveal key elements that impact the implementation and evolution of medical AI solutions. It is essential to see AI as a support tool rather than a substitute for human expertise, as shown by Chi Mei Hospital. By involving multiple teams and fostering collaborative projects focused on specific clinical needs, resistance to AI integration can be reduced, making it easier to integrate into health processes.

In addition, support from information services (ISs) is critical to the successful development of artificial intelligence initiatives in the healthcare field. However, high workloads may hinder their ability to provide sufficient assistance. To meet this challenge, Chi Mei Hospital has set a budget for data processing fees, encouraging IT experts to participate in artificial intelligence projects outside their normal working hours. This approach has been successful in gaining the internal support and expertise needed to advance AI efforts in healthcare.

The experiments also highlight the importance of involving patients from the beginning and in a diverse way during the design phase of AI-advanced healthcare solutions. Training on AI technologies before seeking patient feedback promotes meaningful engagement and ensures that solutions meet the needs of patients. Patient education is essential for building confidence and acceptance of AI-based medical interventions, which ultimately leads to improved patient outcomes.

This understanding highlights the importance of cooperation between stakeholders, transparent communication regarding the role of artificial intelligence in health, and proactive strategies to address organizational challenges related to resource constraints and data management. By using lessons learned from previous implementations, healthcare providers can better manage the challenges of implementing and expanding AI systems, paving the way for transformative advances in patient management. See references: (Liu et al., 2021) and (Trisotech et al., 2024).

2.8 Future Trends in AI Scalability for Healthcare

2.8.1 The Impact of Emerging Technologies on Scalability

New medical AI technologies are dramatically transforming the growth capacity of systems and services. A significant advance is the integration of broad language models (LLMs) into artificial intelligence frameworks, as shown by a recent collaboration between the Healthcare Triangle and a major health system. This integration allows for a better understanding and analysis of natural language, which strengthens the capabilities of artificial intelligence systems in healthcare settings.

In addition, advances in artificial intelligence computing accelerators such as GPUs, TPUs, and FPGAs are optimizing the performance of AI models to process medical data quickly with minimal delay. Accelerators promise faster detection, more effective treatment planning, and improved analysis, all of which contribute to better quality patient care. Customizing these IT solutions to meet specific healthcare needs is a critical step toward improving the efficiency and accessibility of AI-based healthcare innovations.

The fusion of artificial intelligence with Internet of Things (IoT) devices and connected devices is another major trend that has considerable potential for real-time health monitoring. By integrating artificial intelligence algorithms into wristband technology, healthcare professionals can continuously monitor healthcare data, make proactive recommendations, and issue alerts when necessary. This combination not only improves patient monitoring but also allows for the creation of personalized management plans based on the basis of ongoing healthcare data. This is a major turning point in the approach of artificial intelligence to scalability in healthcare. By using LLMs, advanced IT accelerators, and IoT integrations, healthcare organizations can improve their operational efficiency, enhance patient outcomes, and pave the way for a more personalized healthcare delivery model as shown in Table 2.3. See references: (Varnosfaderani & Forouzanfar, 2024) and (Healthcare Triangle, 2024).

2.8.2 Predictions for the Future Landscape

The future of AI scalability in healthcare is making great strides, supported by several key trends. One major phenomenon is the integration of artificial intelligence with the Internet of Things (IoT) and bespoke technology, which promises to transform real-time health monitoring systems. This combination enables proactive health management through personalized advice and alerts, allowing users to discover health and performance indicators that improve their overall well-being.

In addition, advances in medical imaging enriched by artificial intelligence are expected to provide more advanced techniques that deliver sharper and more accurate images. This improvement will allow for the early identification of diseases, enabling healthcare providers to identify potential health

Table 2.3 Emerging trends and potential impacts of AI in healthcare

Trend/Application	Potential impact	Challenges	Future directions
Personalized medicine	Revolutionizes treatment for diseases with genetic components, significantly improving patient outcomes through customized care plans	Data privacy, integration into clinical practice, and ensuring equitable access across diverse patient populations	Extending personalized medicine to include mental health, lifestyle disorders, and the integration of real-time health monitoring data for adaptive treatment modifications
AI-powered tools for health and sleep monitoring	Improved detection and diagnosis of sleep disorders, early identification of potential health issues, personalized treatment, and proactive interventions	Data privacy, accuracy of predictions, and user acceptance and comfort with interventional technologies	Developing analytical and intervention technologies to monitor, anticipate, and manage health concerns and sleep disorders; integrating with wearable devices and smart home technology for real-time modifications
Longevity and aging	Unlocks new possibilities in aging research, promoting healthier, extended lifespans through AI-driven genomic interventions and predictive analytics for preventive medicine	Addressing ethical implications of longevity research, ensuring accessibility and fairness in anti-aging treatments	Leveraging AI for comprehensive health longevity platforms, integrating AI with regenerative medicine, and creating personalized anti-aging treatment plans based on predictive health analytics
AI in drug discovery and development	Reduces time and costs in drug market introduction and enhances the efficacy of new drugs by identifying optimal candidate molecules	Ensuring the reliability of AI predictions and addressing ethical concerns around automated decision-making in drug development	Leveraging AI to explore novel drug pathways, improve clinical trial design, and predict patient responses to treatments more accurately
Advanced robotics in surgery and rehabilitation	Improves precision in surgeries and patient outcomes in rehabilitation, potentially reducing recovery times and healthcare costs	Ethical considerations include the autonomy of robotic systems and the need for robust training programs for medical staff. Current research focuses on robotic systems	Developing autonomous surgical robots, enhancing robotic systems with sensory feedback for improved rehabilitation outcomes, and expanding applications in minimally invasive procedures

AI hardware accelerators	Faster diagnoses, treatment planning, and analysis, improved patient care outcomes, and real-time medical data processing	Integration with medical devices; cost and power consumption of accelerators	Develop healthcare-specific AI hardware; improve accessibility of AI-driven healthcare
AI-enhanced medical imaging	Enables earlier and more accurate disease detection, potentially even identifying health risks before symptoms appear, thus shifting toward preventive healthcare models	Balancing the need for patient privacy with the benefits of data sharing for AI training; integrating AI tools with existing healthcare infrastructures	Developing AI systems capable of cross-modality analysis, improving 3D imaging techniques, and creating predictive models for disease progression based on imaging data
Integrating AI with IoT and wearables	Leads to proactive health management and personalized health recommendations, potentially reducing emergency healthcare interventions	Addressing data security and ensuring device interoperability across different healthcare systems	Improving predictive analytics for the early identification of health anomalies, establishing a network of interconnected devices for comprehensive health monitoring; discreet health surveillance
Enhancing patient outcomes and system efficiency	Promises significant improvements in patient care through earlier disease detection, customized treatments, and optimized healthcare resource management	Ensuring equitable improvements across all populations, addressing the digital divide in healthcare access	Integrating AI-based health advisories into public health plans, refining healthcare delivery models through predictive resource allocation, and improving remote patient monitoring systems
Global health monitoring systems	Strengthens global health security by enabling rapid responses to disease outbreaks and guiding public health interventions with data-driven insights	Integrating diverse data streams in real time, and adapting models quickly to emerging health threats	Establishing global AI-enhanced surveillance systems, improve predictive models for epidemic and pandemic forecasting, and develop AI-driven platforms for vaccine and treatment innovation

(Continued)

Table 2.3 Emerging trends and potential impacts of AI in healthcare (*Continued*)

Trend/Application	Potential impact	Challenges	Future directions
Addressing data scarcity	Facilitates AI development in under-researched areas, such as rare diseases, by making efficient use of limited data resources	Creating effective models with sparse data ensures the generalizability of findings from limited datasets	Investigating innovative data augmentation methods, utilizing crowdsourcing for data acquisition, and promoting cross-institutional data sharing activities enhance datasets. Formulating sophisticated methodologies grounded in few-shot learning
Ensuring model versatility	Allows for the broader application of AI models across varying healthcare settings and patient demographics, improving the universality and accessibility of AI-driven healthcare solutions	Developing adaptable models that maintain high accuracy across diverse datasets addresses potential biases in AI training	Advancing transfer learning and domain adaptation techniques that can be personalized at the point of care
Ensuring data privacy	Enhances privacy and security in healthcare applications, addressing one of the major concerns of digital health data management	Balancing the utility of data for AI training with stringent privacy requirements, adapting regulations to keep pace with technological advancements	Developing more advanced privacy-preserving AI techniques, such as secure multiparty computation, federated learning, and advanced encryption methods for health data
Stakeholder acceptance	Successful AI integration in healthcare, leading to improved trust and collaboration	Concerns about AI reliability and clinician autonomy	Transparent communication and training programs
Building trust with Explainable AI (XAI)	Enhances the trustworthiness of AI systems among healthcare professionals and patients, ensuring that AI-supported decisions are well-informed and ethically sound	Simplifying complex AI decision-making processes for non-technical stakeholders, ensuring explanations are meaningful and actionable	Integrating XAI into clinical workflows, developing standards for AI explanations in healthcare, and educating healthcare professionals on interpreting AI decisions

Source: Reference (Varmosfaderani & Forouzanfar, 2024)

risks before symptoms appear. This transition to preventive health models is expected to result in improved patient outcomes. An improvement in the efficiency and accessibility of healthcare solutions based on artificial intelligence is also expected with AI hardware accelerators. Using specialized technologies such as GPUs, TPUs and FPGAs to improve the performance of AI models, it is possible to perform real-time manipulation of medical data with minimal latency. This capacity will lead to faster diagnosis, treatment planning, and analyses, which will ultimately improve patient management.

In summary, the evolving landscape of AI scalability in healthcare places emphasis on advances in personalized support, advanced diagnostics, and improved treatment outcomes. Collaboration between artificial intelligence and emerging technologies such as the IoT and connected devices, advances in medical imaging via artificial intelligence, and advances in dedicated system accelerators collectively herald a new era of transformative care delivery. See references: (Varnosfaderani & Forouzanfar, 2024), (Oikonomou & Khera, 2024), and (Cloud Computing in Healthcare Landscape Key Benefits of Cloud Computing for Healthcare Providers Real-World Applica, 2024).

2.9 Conclusion

In summary, to achieve an effective adaptation of artificial intelligence in the field of healthcare, it is necessary to adopt a comprehensive approach that addresses various challenges related to data management, model implementation, infrastructure optimization, and operational efficiency. According to the study, integrating artificial intelligence into medical procedures requires more than just technological advances; it also requires a cultural shift that sees artificial intelligence as a tool to improve care delivery and generate new opportunities.

Clear regulatory frameworks are crucial to building trust, ensuring safety, and guiding the ethical use of artificial intelligence in healthcare. Investing in human skills development, continuing education, and fostering a supportive environment are essential to effectively integrate artificial intelligence systems. In addition, optimizing infrastructure requirements and using cloud solutions can improve capacity for growth while maintaining data security and privacy.

The implementation of optimization methods to improve the scalability of artificial intelligence systems in the field of healthcare involves the ethical and secure application of artificial intelligence. Successful case studies highlight the benefits of using large-scale artificial intelligence in medical environments, emphasizing the importance of learning from past experiences.

In perspective, emerging new technologies will continue to define the capacity for growth in medical artificial intelligence, impacting the future of medical practices. The transformative potential of medical personalization, new drug discovery, and improved patient management is highlighted by the predictions. By engaging responsibly with AI technologies and proactively addressing key challenges, healthcare institutions can discover great benefits while reducing risks See references: (Liu et al., 2021), (Esmaeilzadeh, 2024), (Hasan, 2023), and (Spatharou et al., 2020).

References

AI Implementation in Healthcare: 10 Challenges and Solutions. (2024). https:// www.scalefocus.com/blog/ai-implementation-in-healthcare-10-challenges-and -solutions

Alifia Hasan. (2023). Empowering Healthcare with Responsible AI: Scaling and Fortifying a Community of Practice. https://dihi.org/empowering-healthcare-with -responsible-ai-scaling-and-fortifying-a-community-of-practice/

Broshkov, D. (2024). Benefits of Using the Google Cloud Healthcare Platform. https:// zenbit.tech/blog/benefits-of-google-cloud-platform/

Chinthakunta, A. (2024). Transforming Healthcare: The Role of AI in Enhancing the Patient Experience. https://blog.lumen.com/transforming-healthcare-the-role-of-ai -in-enhancing-the-patient-experience/

Cloud Computing in Healthcare Landscape Key Benefits of Cloud Computing for Healthcare Providers Real-World Applica. (2024). https://www.netguru.com/blog /cloud-computing-in-healthcare

Cloud Computing in Healthcare: Top 9 Benefits Revealed | Symphony Solutions. (2024). https://symphony-solutions.com/insights/benefits-of-cloud-computing-in -healthcare

Cohen, R. Y., & Kovacheva, V. P. (2023). A methodology for a scalable, collaborative, and resource-efficient platform, MERLIN, to facilitate healthcare AI research. *IEEE Journal of Biomedical and Health Informatics*, 27(6), 3014–3025.

Dash, S., Shakyawar, S. K., Sharma, M., & Kaushik, S. (2019). Big data in healthcare: Management, analysis and future prospects. *Journal of Big Data*, 6(1), 1–25.

Esmaeilzadeh, P. (2024). Challenges and strategies for wide-scale artificial intelligence (AI) deployment in healthcare practices: A perspective for healthcare organizations. *Artificial Intelligence in Medicine*, 151, 102861.

Healthcare Triangle. Inc. (2024). Healthcare Triangle Breaks New Ground in AI-Powered Patient Data Management with readabl.ai. https://www.globenewswire .com/news-release/2024/04/03/2856851/0/en/Healthcare-Triangle-Breaks-New -Ground-in-AI-Powered-Patient-Data-Management-with-readabl-ai.html

Kasyapa, M. S., & Vanmathi, C. (2024). Blockchain integration in healthcare: A comprehensive investigation of use cases, performance issues, and mitigation strategies. *Frontiers in Digital Health*, 6. https://doi.org/10.3389/fdgth.2024 .1359858

KMS Staff. (2024). Healthcare Data Management: Benefits, Challenges, and Best Practices. https://kms-healthcare.com/blog/healthcare-data-management/

Lee, E. E., Torous, J., De Choudhury, M., Depp, C. A., Graham, S. A., Kim, H. C., & Jeste, D. V. (2021). Artificial intelligence for mental health care: Clinical applications, barriers, facilitators, and artificial wisdom. *Biological Psychiatry: Cognitive Neuroscience and Neuroimaging*, 6(9), 856–864.

Liu, C. F., Huang, C. C., Wang, J. J., Kuo, K. M., & Chen, C. J. (2021, June). The Critical Factors Affecting the Deployment and Scaling of Healthcare AI: Viewpoint from an Experienced Medical Center. In *Healthcare* (Vol. 9, No. 6). Multidisciplinary Digital Publishing Institute (MDPI).

Mennella, C., Maniscalco, U., De Pietro, G., & Esposito, M. (2024). Ethical and regulatory challenges of AI technologies in healthcare: A narrative review. *Heliyon*, 10(4), e26297.

Merkow, J., Dorfner, F. J., Yang, X., Ersoy, A., Dasegowda, G., Kalra, M., & Tarapov, I. (2024). Scalable drift monitoring in medical imaging AI. *arXiv preprint arXiv:2410.13174.*

Oikonomou, E. K., & Khera, R. (2024). Designing medical artificial intelligence systems for global use: Focus on interoperability, scalability, and accessibility. *Hellenic Journal of Cardiology.* https://doi.org/10.1016/j.hjc.2024.07.003

sdettech. (2024). Scalability Challenges and Solutions in Healthcare Insurance Systems. https://sdettech.com/scalability-challenges-and-solutions-in-healthcare-insurance-systems/

Simon Barr. (2024). AI Scalability and Customization: How Can AI Fit in Your Healthcare. https://bhmpc.com/2024/09/ai-scalability-and-customization-how-can-ai-fit-in-your-healthcare-administration/

Spatharou, A., Hieronimus, S., & Jenkins, J. (2020). Transforming healthcare with AI: The impact on the workforce and organizations. https://www.mckinsey.com/industries/healthcare/our-insights/transforming-healthcare-with-ai

Tawalbeh, L. A., & Habeeb, S. (2018). An integrated cloud-based healthcare system. Proceedings of the 2018 Fifth International Conference on Internet of Things: Systems, Management and Security (IoTSMS), Valencia, Spain, 268–273. https://doi.org/10.1109/IoTSMS.2018.8554648

Trisotech, http://www.facebook.com/trisotech. (2024). Healthcare - Industry - Trisotech. https://www.trisotech.com/healthcare/

Varnosfaderani, S. M., & Forouzanfar, M. (2024). The role of AI in hospitals and clinics: Transforming healthcare in the 21st century. *Bioengineering, 11*(4). https://doi.org/10.3390/bioengineering11040337

Vultr Industry Cloud Solutions – Healthcare and Life Sciences - Vultr. (2024). https://www.vultr.com/solutions/healthcare-life-sciences/

Wen, A., Fu, S., Moon, S., Wazir, M. E., Rosenbaum, A., & Kaggal, V. C. (2019). Desiderata for delivering NLP to accelerate healthcare AI advancement and a Mayo Clinic NLP-as-a-service implementation. NPJ Digital Medicine, 2(1), 1–10. https://doi.org/10.1038/s41746-019-0121-0

Williams, E., Kienast, M., Medawar, E., Reinelt, J., Merola, A., Klopfenstein, S. A. I., & Niehaus, S. (2023). A standardized clinical data harmonization pipeline for scalable AI application deployment (FHIR-DHP): Validation and usability study. *JMIR medical informatics, 11,* e43847.

3 Architectures for Scalable AI in Healthcare

Houneida Sakly, Ramzi Guetari, Naoufel Kraiem, and Mourad Abed

3.1 Introduction

3.1.1 Overview of Scalable AI in Healthcare

The development of scalable AI in health is essential to address the challenges of scalability, security, and efficiency in today's healthcare systems. Advanced technologies such as blockchain and hybrid deep learning have become transformative tools for health data management. Blockchain offers a decentralized and immutable registry that enhances the security and clarity of data transactions while preserving their integrity and confidentiality. By integrating blockchain with hybrid deep learning methods, healthcare institutions can make processing, analysis, and decision-making tasks more flexible and secure.

This innovative approach improves capacity for growth by distributing data processing tasks to multiple nodes via techniques such as networked learning and remote computing. This distribution increases transaction speed while ensuring data privacy through advanced encryption methods and anomaly detection models. Deep learning algorithms improve data processing capabilities by detecting patterns, anticipating outcomes, and performing analytical tasks more effectively. In addition, the combination of deep learning with blockchain allows for the shared exploitation of medical data, which further promotes scalability.

The decentralized nature of blockchain allows for a smooth exchange of data between different healthcare systems, effectively solving interoperability issues often encountered by traditional networks. Adopting smart contracts and standardized data formats promotes collaboration between healthcare providers while preserving patient privacy.

Practical applications have highlighted the practicality and benefits of this framework, particularly in terms of scalability, security, and data-driven decision-making. Ongoing research, partnerships, and concrete implementation are essential to promote this innovative approach to healthcare. Exploring new technologies such as cloud computing can further improve the performance and efficiency of scalable AI architectures and benchmarking as described in Table 3.1 health systems.

DOI: 10.1201/9781003480594-3

Table 3.1 Benchmark model approaches, issues, problems, and research gaps

Benchmark model approach	Issues	Problems	Research gaps
MedRec[1]	Limited scalability due to centralized architecture	Lack of privacy and data confidentiality mechanisms	Developing efficient decentralized consensus algorithms for scalability and enhancing privacy-preserving techniques
MedChain[2]	Reliance on trusted intermediaries for validation	Vulnerability to single point of failure	Exploring alternative decentralized validation mechanisms and fault-tolerant approaches
MedBlocks[3]	Lack of interoperability and standardization across healthcare systems	Difficulty in integrating legacy systems with blockchain infrastructure	Investigating interoperability solutions and methods for seamless integration

Source: Reference (Ali et al., 2023)
[1] https://medrec-m.com
[2] https://medchain.pro
[3] https://medblocks.com

Scalable AI has considerable potential to transform health systems by improving data management, facilitating secure data exchange, and improving patient outcomes. The alliance between blockchain technology and hybrid deep learning is a promising way to increase capacity for growth while preserving data privacy and security in contemporary healthcare environments. See reference: (Ali et al., 2023).

3.1.2 Importance of Scalable Architectures

The key role of scalable infrastructures is to promote AI applications in the health field. Healthcare institutions can effectively manage their AI tasks, reduce delays, and ensure compliance with regulations through their ability to adapt. Using adaptive infrastructures, such as those offered by Cloud GPUs and the Kubernetes Engine, which are equipped with AMD and NVIDIA accelerators, healthcare providers can offer personalized, genetic, and diagnostic assistance while maintaining the location of the data.

The importance of scalable infrastructures lies in their flexibility and modular design. By integrating microservices, health AI systems can achieve greater modularity, making it easier to create, test, and deploy new functionalities. Containerization also increases efficiency by encapsulating AI components and their dependencies, allowing for smooth deployment in various environments. Scalable AI infrastructures require cloud computing, which offers flexible deployment options and efficient data management services for healthcare applications.

In addition, fog and edge computing technologies improve the performance of medical artificial intelligence systems by enabling real-time analysis, improving data privacy, and ensuring secure connections between devices. The key role of scalable infrastructures is to promote applications

By effectively balancing IT resources and optimizing storage management strategies, healthcare organizations can improve the overall performance of their scalable AI infrastructures. Real-time processing capabilities are essential for health applications to analyze data quickly and make informed, accurate decisions.

In summary, adaptive infrastructures are essential for the successful integration of AI into the health field. By using microservices for modularity, containerization for efficiency, cloud computing for deployment flexibility, and fog and edge computing for performance improvement, as well as optimizing IT resources and storage management strategies, healthcare institutions can develop robust artificial intelligence systems that effectively deliver real-time insights and personalized support. See references: (AI Scalability in Health Solutions, 2024) and (Vultr Industry Cloud Solutions – Healthcare and Life Sciences – Vultr, 2024).

3.2   Microservices for Modularity

3.2.1   Definition and Benefits of Microservices

Modularity plays a key role in the development of scalable architectures for AI health systems. Microservices, which are designed to be modular, play an important role in creating individual components that can be easily updated and maintained without disrupting the entire system. Microservices in AI for health purposes enable better data collection, cohort training, and model training procedures.

After the system is broken into small departments, AI platforms in health can effectively solve challenges related to data translation, cohort creation, and model building. This method allows for continuous improvement of data cohorts and models, leading to more efficient and productive medical AI solutions. Microservices make it easier to manage large volumes of medical records and multimodal data.

A great advantage of microservices is their ability to be extended. These services can be used independently, allowing horizontal expansion on the basis of demand. As medical data increases in size and complexity, extending each component as needed to maintain optimal system performance is essential.

In addition, microservices increase system reliability by preventing failures within certain services rather than affecting them across the platform. This isolation ensures that any problem can be quickly resolved without disrupting other parts of the system. In summary, integrating microservices into medical artificial intelligence architectures has many benefits, such as modularity, scalability, reliability, and better data management. By effectively leveraging these services, healthcare companies can accelerate the evolution of AI models and thus improve patient care. See references: (Autonomous Systems Healthcare AI Solutions, 2024) and (Hossain et al., 2023).

3.2.2 Implementation of Microservices in Healthcare AI Systems

Microservices play a critical role in the integration of scalable artificial intelligence into the health sector. By dividing complex applications into small stand-alone services, microservices promote modularity, flexibility, and the ability to be expanded. With this approach, AI medical teams can develop, implement, and extend their services independently, leading to more efficient and impactful data flow solutions.

In the context of edge computing and fog computing environments, microservices provide an efficient solution for managing IoT applications. A key element for health artificial intelligence systems is moving from old monolithic architectures to those based on microservices. By using lightweight virtualization and containerization technologies, microservices can facilitate the secure and automated deployment of AI-driven applications at the network edge.

It is essential not to overlook the security concerns associated with the deployment of microservices at the edge of the IoT. Addressing privacy issues is critical when implementing microservices at this level to create reliable decision-making infrastructures. Using containerization technology within edge computing-based microservice frameworks can help solve these security challenges.

In summary, the adoption of microservices in health AI systems can significantly improve the efficiency and effectiveness of operations. By adopting modularization through microservices, organizations can better meet the demands of contemporary AI applications while ensuring flexibility and resilience. See references: (Cohen & Kovacheva, 2023), (Autonomous Systems Healthcare AI Solutions, 2024), and (Hossain et al., 2023).

3.3 Containerization for Efficiency

3.3.1 Understanding Containers in AI Architecture

In regard to the AI architecture, understanding the concept of containerization is essential for effectively implementing AI models. Using containerization tools such as Docker and Kubernetes, we simplify the deployment process by consolidating the application code and its dependencies into lightweight, portable modules. This method allows smooth operation across different computer environments, which results in improved scalability, management, and portability of artificial intelligence systems.

By integrating containerization into AI architecture, companies can benefit from greater flexibility in managing and organizing their applications. Containers allow for easy adaptation of AI tasks across various devices and nodes, resulting in more efficient use of resources. This results in improved performance of AI applications and smooth management of complex AI systems in healthcare.

In addition, containerization promotes the efficient use of IT resources by separating applications within containers, which avoids conflicts and ensures consistent performance. With the ability to manage multiple containers on a single host machine, companies can efficiently optimize their computing resources while maintaining the performance needed for AI applications in health.

In summary, the integration of containerization into the AI architecture provides a solid solution to improve the efficiency, scalability, and flexibility when medical artificial intelligence systems are implemented. By using container technologies, companies can simplify their operations, improve resource deployment, and ensure consistent performance across different computing environments, as seen in Figure 3.1 and Table 3.2. See reference: (AI, 2024).

3.3.2   Advantages of Containerization in Healthcare Applications

The integration of containerization is a major change in the health application revolution, offering many benefits. A key advantage is the ability to deploy lightweight and portable applications on landmarks and devices. Using technologies such as Docker and Kubernetes, it is possible to deploy applications

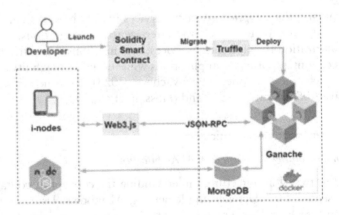

Figure 3.1 Simulation environment (Alsaeed et al., 2024).

Table 3.2 Comparison of our survey with existing related surveys

Research domain	References	Year	Infrastructure	Methods	Machine learning	Resource management	ML model sizing	Heterogeneity	Security	Scheduling	Container migration	Container scaling
Edge AI Scaling Challenges (2022)	Ali et al., 2023; AI Scalability in Health Solutions, 2024; Rathi et al., 2021	2022	Cloud	Heuristic	Machine Learning	Resource Allocation	Reduced	Computational	Platform	Container	Stateful vs. Stateless containers	Proactive vs. reactive scaling decisions
Edge AI Frameworks (2023)	Edge AI: A Taxonomy, Systematic Review and Future Directions, 2024; Cloud Computing in Healthcare: Top 9 Benefits Revealed I Symphony Solutions, 2024; Revolutionizing Healthcare: The Impact of Cloud Computing and Artificial Intelligence, 2024; Cohen et al., 2023; Fx is Ai, 2024	2023	Cloud, Edge	Meta-Heuristic	Machine Learning	Application Placement, Workload Distribution	Full, Reduced	Computational, Host Hardware	Host	Service	Inter- vs. intracluster migrations	Horizontal, Vertical, and Hybrid scaling
AI Model Deployment (2024)	Jeyaraman et al., 2024; Vultr Industry Cloud Solutions – Healthcare and Life Sciences – Vultr, 2024; How Edge Computing Improves Data Processing Speed and Efficiency in Healthcare, 2024	2024	Cloud, Fog, Edge		Deep Reinforcement Learning	ML Model Sizing (Full & Reduced)	Computational	Platform	Pod	Migrations at Cloud/Edge/Fog	Simulations vs. real-world testbed migrations
AI-Based Healthcare Applications	AI Scalability in Health Solutions, 2024; Cloud Computing in Healthcare: Top 9 Benefits Revealed I Symphony Solutions, 2024; Revolutionizing Healthcare: The Impact of Cloud Computing and Artificial Intelligence, 2024	2020-2023	Cloud, Edge	Heuristic, Machine Learning, Meta-Heuristic	Application Placement	Computational, Hardware	Platform			Reactive, proactive		

(Edge AI: A Taxonomy, Systematic Review and Future Directions, 2024)

seamlessly, which facilitates the management, orchestration, and scalability of AI systems in health. This portability and flexibility allows healthcare providers to effectively manage their applications in different environments.

In addition, containerization significantly improves resource utilization and efficiency in health applications. By encapsulating application code and dependencies in a single, isolated unit, containers ensure consistent performance across different computing environments. This consistency ensures that medical AI systems operate smoothly and reliably, regardless of the underlying infrastructure.

Another major benefit of containerization in health applications is its improved safety. The isolation of applications inside containers reduces potential security risks by avoiding interference between different system elements. This isolation also allows for better control of access permissions and data confidentiality, which are essential considerations in the sensitive health sector. In addition, containerization facilitates the implementation of artificial intelligence systems for health. Containers can be easily replicated and deployed across multiple nodes or devices, allowing for perfect scalability on demand. This scalability allows healthcare providers to cope with increased data volumes and computing needs without compromising system performance. In summary, containerization offers many benefits for healthcare applications by enabling portability, resource efficiency, improved security, and simplified scalability. By using container technologies such as Docker and Kubernetes, healthcare companies can optimize their AI systems to improve performance and adaptability in an ever-changing digital health environment. See references: (Alsaeed et al., 2024) and (George et al., 2023).

3.4 Cloud Computing for Flexible Deployment

3.4.1 Role of Cloud Computing in Scalable AI Architectures

Cloud computing has transformed the scalability of AI frameworks in healthcare. By utilizing a secure and adaptable cloud infrastructure, healthcare businesses can effectively handle substantial data volumes, leading to enhanced operational efficiency and superior patient management. This technology facilitates healthcare practitioners' access to patient medical records, hence enhancing teamwork and enabling individualized treatment options informed by past data. (Aceto et al., 2020)

A significant benefit of cloud computing is the equitable dissemination of medical data, which enables people to assume control of their health information and engage actively in their health management. Digital platforms enable access to medical records, promoting patient engagement in health management. Moreover, cloud technology enables the incorporation of IoT solutions into healthcare operations, enhancing the visibility of patient pathways and ensuring access to essential medical data across various devices.

Cloud computing also facilitates the integration of artificial intelligence and machine learning applications into healthcare systems, enabling advanced analytics and personalized health approaches. By using AI algorithms on cloud platforms to analyze a large amount of medical data, providers can make informed decisions that lead to better patient outcomes. As the healthcare industry increasingly adopts cloud computing technologies, the benefits exceed those of individual businesses. Scalable AI architectures are transforming the delivery and management of medical services by leveraging the benefits of modern technologies such as cloud computing.

By adopting scalable cloud solutions such as Vultr's Cloud GPU with the Kubernetes Engine to manage artificial intelligence workloads, health care companies can maintain regulatory compliance while supporting personalized care initiatives such as genetics and diagnostics. The flexibility offered by composable infrastructure allows organizations to adapt effectively to evolving demands without being limited to specific vendors.

Cloud computing solutions as shown in Table 3.3 plays a critical role in the adoption of scalable AI systems in the health sector by providing secure data management, improving operational efficiency, improving patient outcomes, and reducing costs. As technology continues to evolve, the integration of cloud-based solutions with artificial intelligence applications will be crucial in shaping the future of care delivery. See references: (Cloud Computing

Table 3.3 Autoscaling techniques used by various cloud providers

Cloud providers	AutoScaling Feature	AutoScaling Supported (Yes/No)
AMAZON	Automatically scales number of EC2 instances for different applications.	Yes
WINDOWS AZURE	Provides autoscaling feature manually based on the applications	Yes
GOOGLE APP	Owns autoscaling technology.	Yes
ENGINE	Google applications.	Yes
GOGRID	Supports autoscaling technique in a programmatic way but does not implement it.	Yes/No
FLEXISCALE	Provides autoscaling mechanism with high performance and availability.	Yes
ANEKA	Application management service through cloud peer service.	Yes
NIMBUS	Open-source cloud provided by resource manager and Python modules.	Yes
EUCALYPTUS	Open-source cloud which provides wrapper service for various applications.	Yes
OPEN NEBULA	Open-source cloud which provides OpenNebula Service Management Project.	Yes

(Alharthi et al., 2024)

in Healthcare Landscape Key Benefits of Cloud Computing for Healthcare Providers Real-World Applications, 2024) and (Vultr Industry Cloud Solutions – Healthcare and Life Sciences – Vultr, 2024).

3.4.2 Cloud Services for Healthcare Data Management

Cloud services play a critical role in medical data management by providing flexible and secure solutions for storing, managing, and processing medical information. A key element of cloud computing in healthcare is the ability to scale IT resources efficiently. This flexibility allows healthcare organizations to adapt quickly to changing situations, such as outbreaks or peak demand, without being constrained by traditional onsite servers. Cloud computing allows clinics to expand or contract as needed, optimizing expenses while ensuring quality service.

In addition, online storage solutions allow for a smooth flow of data, ensuring the security of medical records and their easy accessibility to authorized users from any device connected to the internet. Regular updates help maintain the accuracy and consistency of medical data while improving interoperability to facilitate integration across different health systems. Effective access to medical records facilitates collaboration between care providers and allows for the creation of personalized treatment plans on the basis of historical patient data.

Cloud computing also makes medical data more accessible by allowing patients to manage their health information, access their records at any time, and actively participate in their well-being. This transparency in patient journeys promotes proactive health management and improves the overall patient experience. As cloud technology continues to evolve, its impact on medical data management will be significant. Through the use of cloud services for medical data management, companies can improve their efficiency, enhance the delivery of patient care, reduce difficulties and operating costs, and stimulate innovation in the creation of new health solutions. See references: (Cloud Computing in Healthcare Landscape Key Benefits of Cloud Computing for Healthcare Providers Real-World Applications, 2024).

3.5 Fog and Edge Computing for Enhanced Performance

3.5.1 Differentiating Fog and Edge Computing

Edge computing and fog computing are two distinct paradigms that play critical roles in improving data processing capabilities across various sectors, including the health sector. Although both are intended to bring digital resources closer to the data source, they have distinctive features that distinguish them.

Edge computing uses a decentralized infrastructure to process data at or near the source, reducing latency and conserving bandwidth. This method is gaining popularity in the health field because of its potential to improve real-time decision-making and decision-making in critical medical situations. By enabling onsite data analysis, edge computing is essential for urgent diagnostics, such as heart attack detection and during care, which allows immediate assessment of vital signs and physiological parameters to ensure patient safety. In chronic disease management, continuous data collection through portable devices facilitates proactive disease management and rapid adjustments to treatment plans. Fog computing aims to bring IT resources closer to the data source than edge computing does. This method processes data directly on IoT devices or gateways, avoiding the need to transmit information to a centralized cloud or analytics server. In healthcare applications, fog computing enables real-time processing of patient data at the device scale, resulting in reduced latency and faster response. For example, in remote patient monitoring systems, this technology can remotely analyze vital signs and issue alerts only when necessary, reducing unnecessary data transmission.

Although fog computing works slightly further from the device than edge computing does, it still has advantages such as reduced latency compared with traditional cloud-based methods. Edge computing, on the other hand, offers even lower latency by processing data directly on devices or gateways. Each paradigm has its own strengths and is well-suited to a variety of health situations.

By understanding the distinctions between fog computing and edge computing, healthcare companies can strategically implement this technology to improve diagnostic accuracy, improve patient monitoring capabilities, and provide effective personalized treatments as seen in Figure 3.2 and Table 3.4. See references: (Jeyaraman et al., 2024), (Jeyaraman et al., 2024), and (Edge AI: A Taxonomy, Systematic Review and Future Directions, 2024), (Gill et al., 2024).

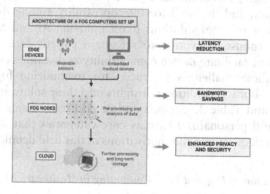

Figure 3.2 Architecture and advantages of the fog computing model (Jeyaraman et al., 2024)

Table 3.4 Comparison of cloud computing and fog computing in healthcare

Feature	Cloud computing	Fog computing
Data processing location	Centralized in remote data centers	Decentralized, at or near the source of data
Latency	Higher due to the longer distance data travels	Lower, as data is processed closer to their origin
Bandwidth usage	Higher, as large amounts of data are transmitted to and from the cloud	Lower, due to local data processing and reduced data transmission
Real-time capability	Limited by network latency	Enhanced, suitable for time-sensitive applications such as emergency response and critical care monitoring
Security risks	Higher, due to extensive data transmission and centralized storage	Reduced, with data processed and often stored locally, minimizing exposure to cyber threats
Interoperability	Dependent on internet and cloud services' protocols	Requires local interoperability standards but is less dependent on external networks
Scalability	Easily scalable with cloud resources	Scalability depends on local infrastructure capabilities
Cost	Potentially lower upfront, with ongoing operational expenses	Higher upfront costs for local infrastructure, potentially lower operational costs

(Jeyaraman et al., 2024)

Distinguishing between fog and edge computing allows healthcare organizations to strategically deploy these technologies, thereby enhancing diagnostic accuracy, real-time patient monitoring, and personalized treatment delivery. However, implementing fog computing in healthcare presents significant challenges, including data privacy concerns, latency management, scalability issues, and the need for interoperability among diverse systems. Addressing these requires solutions like employing AI and ML for predictive analytics, robust encryption to safeguard patient data, and standardized protocols to facilitate device compatibility and seamless data exchange. Overcoming these challenges is crucial for maximizing fog computing's potential in healthcare. Additional insights into these solutions are described in Figure 3.3 and Table 3.5, which outline AI-driven diagnostics, real-time monitoring, and personalized care as core categories that directly address relevant research questions and motivations in this field detailed in Table 3.6.

3.5.2   *Applications of Fog and Edge Computing in Healthcare AI*

Using Fog and edge computing is critical to transforming AI applications into health by bringing data processing capabilities closer together, enabling immediate analysis and rapid decision-making. In the healthcare sector,

Figure 3.3 Challenges with fog computing in healthcare (Jeyaraman et al., 2024).

Table 3.5 Key challenges and proposed solutions for fog computing in healthcare

Challenge	Description	Proposed Solutions
Interoperability	Difficulty in the seamless integration of diverse medical devices and systems	Development and enforcement of universal standards for device communication and data formats
Scalability	Need to handle growing data volumes and device connectivity without performance degradation	Enhance local processing power and develop scalable network architectures
Security	High risk of data breaches and unauthorized access due to decentralized data processing	Implement advanced encryption, use blockchain technology for secure data transactions, and continuous security monitoring
Technical limitations	Limitations in local computational power, especially in remote or resource-limited healthcare settings	Deploy AI and ML to optimize data processing efficiency and manage computational loads
Maintenance	Managing and updating numerous decentralized nodes can be complex and resource-intensive	Utilize sophisticated management tools and skilled personnel, and automate updates and maintenance routines

AI: artificial intelligence; ML: machine learning (Jeyaraman et al., 2024).

Table 3.6 Research questions, motivation, category, and mapping

No.	Research question	Motivation	Category
RQ1	What are the principal techniques and strategies employed in Edge AI, and how do they differ concerning applications, infrastructure, and algorithms?	The purpose of this research question is to understand the various methods and approaches used in Edge AI.	Infrastructure, Application Architecture, and Methods
RQ2	To what extent may heuristic algorithms improve the efficacy and performance of Edge AI systems, particularly in model training and optimization tasks?	This research question helps in examining the role of heuristic methods in Edge AI.	Heuristic Methods
RQ3	What methods do meta-heuristic algorithms employed by Edge AI utilize to address complex optimization challenges, and what are their applications and key attributes?	The characteristics and applications of meta-heuristic methods are investigated in this paper.	Meta-Heuristics Methods
RQ4	In what ways may machine learning approaches, including deep learning models, enhance real-time data processing and decision-making in Edge AI devices?	This research question analyzes the role of ML techniques.	Machine Learning Methods
RQ5	What are the primary advantages and limitations of Edge AI's deep reinforcement learning, particularly in the context of autonomous driving?	The pros and cons of deep reinforcement learning are examined via this research question.	Deep Reinforcement Learning Methods
RQ6	How do Edge AI devices address heterogeneity in computational, hardware, and platform aspects, and what strategies are employed to optimize resource allocation?	Heterogeneity in various aspects is discussed along with optimization of resource allocation approaches.	Heterogeneity and Horizontal, Vertical, and Hybrid container scaling
RQ7	What are the primary problems and strategies for developing Edge AI applications, particularly around resource allocation and task distribution?	The purpose of this research question was to identify challenges and solutions while implementing Edge AI applications.	Resource Provisioning and Workload Distribution and Prediction

(*Continued*)

Table 3.6 (*Continued*)

No.	Research question	Motivation	Category
RQ8	What are the pros and cons of both monolithic and microservices architectures in terms of Edge AI flexibility, performance, and resource utilization?	This research question helps in comparing both monolithic and microservice architectures.	Comparisons of Existing Edge AI approaches on the basis of Application
RQ9	What are the primary factors worth considering for resource management in Edge AI, including resource provisioning, allocation, application placement, workload distribution, and prediction?	The prime factors for resource management are examined through this research question.	Resource Management
RQ10	How do ML model sizing impact the performance and resource consumption of Edge AI applications?	This research question investigates the impact of machine learning model size on the performance and resource consumption of Edge AI applications.	Full ML Model Sizing
RQ11	What are the principal factors influencing the selection of Edge AI infrastructure— namely, Cloud, Fog, and Edge computing— concerning their impact on application performance and resource utilization?	This research question helps identify components that influence the choice of Edge AI infrastructure.	Infrastructure

(Edge AI: A Taxonomy, Systematic Review and Future Directions, 2024)

cloud computing plays a major role in many impactful applications. Real-time stroke detection facilitates rapid detection and management, resulting in reduced long-term disability. During operations, surgical follow-up ensures patient safety by allowing patients to respond quickly to physiological changes. Continuous management of chronic diseases through wearable devices strengthens disease control by providing real-time feedback and treatment adjustments. Telemedicine allows for specialized consultations at a distance, opening the way to access expertise in remote areas. In addition, advanced home care combines the use of fog computing with home health devices to track recovery after hospitalization, reducing readmission rates through personalized follow-up and treatment changes.

Table 3.7 Fog computing applications in healthcare and their impact

Application	Description	Impact on Healthcare
Real-time stroke detection	Processing data from imaging devices in real-time, facilitating rapid diagnosis and treatment	Reduces time to treatment, which is critical for conditions like ischemic strokes, potentially reducing long-term disability
Surgical monitoring	Monitoring and analyzing vital signs and other parameters during surgeries in real time	Enhances patient safety by enabling immediate reactions to physiological changes
Continuous chronic disease management	Using wearable devices to monitor and manage chronic conditions like diabetes in real time	Improves disease management by providing constant feedback and allowing immediate adjustments in treatment
Telemedicine support	Local processing supports real-time communication between remote specialists and patients, facilitating teleconsultations	Expands access to specialist care, particularly in remote areas, improving outcomes by providing timely expert interventions
Advanced home care	Integration of fog computing with home health devices to monitor and manage posthospitalization recovery	Reduces readmission rates by providing continuous, personalized monitoring and adjusting treatments based on real-time data

(Jeyaraman et al., 2024)

This app highlights how cloud computing improves health outcomes by providing accurate interventions and continuous monitoring while optimizing energy consumption for IoT devices. According to the sensitivity analysis, IoT devices equipped with fog nodes always perform better than those without them across various indicators, such as energy costs, idle power, transmitted power and latency. The use of fog and edge computing in medical artificial intelligence highlights the potential to transform patient management by facilitating real-time data manipulation, improving diagnostic accuracy, improving treatment response times and optimizing resource use to improve patient outcomes as described in real applications and their impact in the healthcare sector in Table 3.7. See reference: (Jeyaraman et al., 2024).

3.6   Balancing Compute, Storage, and Networking

3.6.1   *Importance of Optimizing Compute Resources*

Using Fog and edge computing is critical to transforming AI applications into health by bringing data processing capabilities closer together, enabling immediate analysis and rapid decision-making. In the healthcare sector, cloud computing plays a major role in many impactful applications. Real-time stroke detection facilitates rapid detection and management, resulting in reduced long-term disability. During operations, surgical follow-up ensures patient safety by allowing patients to respond quickly to physiological changes. Continuous management of chronic diseases through wearable devices strengthens disease control by providing real-time feedback and treatment adjustments. Telemedicine allows for specialized consultations at a distance, opening the way to access expertise in remote areas. In addition, advanced home care combines the use of fog computing with home health devices to track recovery after hospitalization, reducing readmission rates through personalized follow-up and treatment changes.

This app highlights how cloud computing improves health outcomes by providing accurate interventions and continuous monitoring while optimizing energy consumption for IoT devices. According to the sensitivity analysis, IoT devices equipped with fog nodes always perform better than those without them across various indicators, such as energy costs, idle power, transmitted power and latency. In summary, the use of fog and edge computing in medical artificial intelligence highlights the potential to transform patient management by facilitating real-time data manipulation, improving diagnostic accuracy, improving treatment response times and optimizing resource use to improve patient outcomes as described in Figure 3.4. See reference: (AI scalability in Health Solutions, 2024), (Guo et al., 2024).

3.6.2 Strategies for Efficient Storage Management

It is essential to ensure effective management of data storage in health frameworks. As the amount of data generated by health care institutions continues to grow, it is essential to optimize data retention, access, and processing to ensure smooth operations and performance. An essential means for effective data storage management is to use on-board computing to process the data locally outside the network. This method reduces reliance on centralized cloud servers, reduces latency, and improves responsiveness to real-time data inputs. By processing data closer to its source, edge computing strengthens privacy and security measures while reducing the volume of data to be transmitted over networks. This reduction in data transmission leads to cost

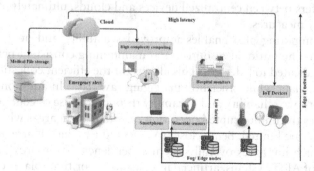

Figure 3.4 Events in each layer of the fog computing model (Jeyaraman et al., 2024).

savings and reduced network congestion, thus facilitating a smoother flow of data. In addition, the use of edge computing allows for easy scalability as the network grows without being constrained by centralized processing capabilities. Another method for effective data storage management involves the use of advanced encryption methods, anomaly detection models, and biomechanical authentication systems to ensure data security in health care systems. By integrating deep learning algorithms into data processing operations, healthcare institutions can analyze large amounts of medical data, identify patterns, anticipate outcomes, and perform analysis tasks more effectively. This optimization speeds up response times and optimizes resource utilization. In addition, the integration of blockchain technology with hybrid deep learning techniques such as federated learning and edge computing can enhance the scalability of medical AI frameworks. This integration allows a decentralized distribution of data processing tasks across multiple nodes and exploits the potential of nearby devices to increase transaction throughput. In reality, adopting methods such as the use of edge computing to process data locally, integrating advanced security measures through deep learning algorithms and integrating blockchain technology to improve scalability are essential advances toward efficient storage management in scalable artificial intelligence architectures for health systems. See references: (How Edge Computing Improves Data Processing Speed and Efficiency in Healthcare, 2024), (Jeyaraman et al., 2024), (Patan, 2024), (Simon, 2024), (Verma et al., 2023) and (Ali et al., 2023).

3.6.3 *Enhancing Networking Capabilities for Performance*

Improving networking skills is crucial to achieving optimal performance in the field of scalable artificial intelligence for health. The use of edge computing is a critical element to consider, as it involves processing data closer to its source, reducing delays, and improving the overall quality of service. By managing data on-premises or in a local data center, edge computing avoids passing information to the computer, allowing immediate responses to user requests. This method also strengthens privacy and data security by reducing data transfers between centralized devices and clouds, ultimately strengthening security measures.

Edge computing also enables improved scalability and adaptability by extending computational resources and maintaining consistent performance through dedicated IoT devices. This allows for the efficient collection of large and diverse data while efficiently managing raw data. In addition, it is possible to improve reliability and durability through the use of edge computing, as it ensures the uninterrupted operation of data even in areas where internet connections are limited. Being closer to users reduces the reliance on core networks, which improves overall system dependency. To improve the energy efficiency of AIoT systems, artificial intelligence algorithms play a critical role in dynamic power distribution and task planning. Using machine learning to manage workload can improve energy efficiency while designing energy-intensive computing components. By integrating renewable energy sources, the efficiency and scalability of systems can be further improved. In addition, advances in secure protocols for remote artificial intelligence and blockchain technology will address privacy issues while ensuring robust and reliable systems. Integrating these network capabilities into scalable AI architectures can significantly improve the performance of health applications while ensuring data security, maintaining confidentiality, and maximizing the efficiency of operations. See references: (How Edge Computing Improves Data Processing Speed and Efficiency in Healthcare, 2024), (Hossain et al., 2023), and (Edge AI: A Taxonomy, Systematic Review and Future Directions, 2024).

3.7 Real-time Processing in Healthcare Applications

3.7.1 Challenges and Solutions for Real-time Data Analysis

Real-time data analysis poses specific challenges in health systems, requiring innovative solutions to achieve optimal results. One of the main challenges is the speed and accuracy of handling large amounts of medical data. As the amount and complexity of data in health systems increase, traditional treatment methods may struggle to provide accurate and effective insights in time.

The issues of privacy and confidentiality further complicate real-time data analysis, as medical data often contains sensitive information that requires protection. It is critical to comply with regulations while allowing for rapid data processing to maintain confidence and security in medical artificial intelligence systems.

Interoperability issues also impact real-time data analysis, as the integration of different health systems and data formats can hinder smooth communication between different elements of the system. Universal standards for the communication of devices and data formats are needed and should be implemented to facilitate the flow of data exchange.

In addition, technical constraints such as the limitation of computing power in remote or resource-limited health environments can impact real-time processing efficiency. Leveraging advanced technologies such as artificial intelligence and machine learning is essential to optimize computing loads and improve processing capabilities in this challenging situation. To address these challenges in real-time data analytics, adopting a holistic approach that integrates flexible architectures, efficient containerization, cloud computing resources, and edge computing capabilities is essential. By effectively balancing computing, storage, and network resources while ensuring regulatory compliance and privacy protection, medical artificial intelligence systems can provide accurate information to improve decision-making and patient management.

In summary, to solve the challenges of real-time data analytics in health applications, a holistic approach that uses leading technologies and industry best practices to ensure efficient operation and accurate and secure health data is needed. See references (Jeyaraman et al., 2024) and (Ali et al., 2023).

3.8 Regulatory Compliance Considerations

When considering the implementation of scalable AI in healthcare, it is essential to comply with regulations to ensure the ethical and legal use of AI technologies. As the health sector becomes increasingly dependent on automation and data processing, it is critical to address challenges related to regulatory frameworks such as the GDPR and the European Union's Artificial Intelligence Act.

One of the top priorities in health AI systems is data security and privacy. Security breaches can cause significant financial and reputational damage to health care companies. The use of edge computing allows sensitive patient data to be processed locally, reducing the risk of breaches when transmitting data across networks. This method not only reduces security vulnerabilities but also ensures compliance with regulations such as HIPAA.

In addition, legal frameworks such as the GDPR and the European artificial intelligence law provide guidelines to preserve data confidentiality and establish access to information in AI decision-making processes. Companies must comply with data protection rules by design and by default, limiting data processing to what is necessary while giving individuals the right to obtain explanations for automated decisions. To address the ethical issues related to algorithmic bias and lack of human control, it is essential that companies have strong management structures that reconcile ethical principles with legal compliance. The EU AI Act implements a risk-based approach that classifies artificial intelligence systems according to their impact on human rights and security. Applications classified as high risk, especially in sectors such as health, are subject to strict regulations to avoid unethical decision-making.

In short, taking into account regulatory compliance is essential to guide companies toward the responsible implementation of scalable artificial intelligence in healthcare environments. By combining ethical principles with legal frameworks, companies can ensure that their artificial intelligence systems work effectively while meeting industry standards and regulatory requirements. See references: (Lin, 2024, pages 1–5) and (Lin, 2024, pages 16–20).

3.9 Conclusions and Future Directions

In the final analysis, the integration of evolving artificial intelligence into health systems opens a promising path to transform patient management and data management. By using scalable structures such as microservices, containerization, cloud computing, and fog/edge computing, healthcare institutions can improve processing responsiveness, decision-making capabilities, and data security. The integration of hybrid deep learning models and blockchain technologies also ensures data sharing security and efficient analysis of health information. The study highlights the importance of exploring innovative consensus mechanisms, privacy preservation techniques, and practical implementations to address regulatory compliance challenges. Ongoing research, collaboration, and hands-on applications are essential for improving the capabilities of evolving artificial intelligence in health systems.

In addition, the strategic adoption of AI technologies in health settings can lead to improvements in the efficiency of care delivery, quality improvements, and strong management structures to ensure ethical use. The potential integration of new technologies such as IoT devices and cloud computing into intelligent medical monitoring systems improves patient outcomes through continuous monitoring and early treatment provision. Addressing the challenges of interoperability, scalability, and security is crucial to fully exploit the transformative potential of cloud computing in healthcare environments. The combination of artificial intelligence and advanced technologies leads to smart health systems that prioritize privacy and security while optimizing decision-making processes. This technology uses genetic encryption for data security, network learning for Internet of Media applications, and nanosensor-equipped systems to improve efficiency. The continued growth of technology-based healthcare solutions highlights the critical importance of scalable AI architectures in designing the future of patient care. See references: (Rathi et al., 2021), (AI Scalability in Health Solutions, 2024), (Edge AI: A Taxonomy, Systematic Review and Future Directions, 2024), (Jeyaraman et al., 2024), (Jeyaraman et al., 2024),(Williams et al., 2023) and (Ali et al., 2023).

References

Aceto, G., Persico, V., & Pescapé, A. (2020). Industry 4.0 and health: Internet of Things, big data, and cloud computing for Healthcare 4.0. *Journal of Industrial Information Integration*, 18, Article 100129. https://doi.org/10.1016/j.jii.2020.100129.

Ali, A., Ali, H., Saeed, A., Ahmed, A., Tin Tin Ting, Assam, M., Yazeed Yasin Ghadi, & Mohamed, H. G. (2023). Blockchain-Powered Healthcare Systems: Enhancing Scalability and Security with Hybrid Deep Learning. *Sensors*, 23(18), 7740–7740. https://doi.org/10.3390/s23187740

Alharthi, S., Alshamsi, A., Alseiari, A., & Alwarafy, A. (2024). AutoScaling Techniques in Cloud Computing: Issues and Research Directions. *Sensors*, 24(17), 5551. https://doi.org/10.3390/s24175551

Alsaeed, N., Nadeem, F., & Faisal Albalwy. (2024). A scalable and lightweight group authentication framework for internet of Medical Things using integrated blockchain and fog computing. *Future Generation Computer Systems*, 151, 162–181. https://doi.org/10.1016/j.future.2023.09.032

AI Scalability in Health Solutions. (2024). https://www.restack.io/p/ai-scalability-knowledge-answer-health-ai-solutions-cat-ai

Autonomous Systems Healthcare AI Solutions. (2024). https://www.restack.io/p/autonomous-systems-answer-healthcare-ai-data-pipeline-cat-ai

Cloud Computing in Healthcare [5 Real Use Cases Included]. (2024). https://acropolium.com/blog/cloud-computing-healthcare/

Cloud Computing in Healthcare Landscape Key Benefits of Cloud Computing for Healthcare Providers Real-World Applications. (2024). https://www.netguru.com /blog/cloud-computing-in-healthcare

Cloud Computing in Healthcare: Top 9 Benefits Revealed | Symphony Solutions. (2024). https://symphony-solutions.com/insights/benefits-of-cloud-computing-in-healthcare

Cohen, R. Y., & Kovacheva, V. P. (2023). A Methodology for A Scalable, Collaborative, And Resource-Efficient Platform, MERLIN, to Facilitate Healthcare AI Research. *IEEE Journal of Biomedical and Health Informatics*, 1–12. https:// doi.org/10.1109/JBHI.2023.3259395

Edge AI: A Taxonomy, Systematic Review and Future Directions. (2024). https:// arxiv.org/html/2407.04053v1

Fx is Ai. (2024). How Does Containerization Help in AI Deployment? https://medium .com/@FxisAi/how-does-containerization-help-in-ai-deployment-e9700f25ac89

George, A. S., George, A. S. Hovan., & Baskar, T. (2023). Edge Computing and the Future of Cloud Computing: A Survey of Industry Perspectives and Predictions. *Zenodo (CERN European Organization for Nuclear Research)*, 2(2). https://doi .org/10.5281/zenodo.8020101

Gill, S. S., Wu, H., Patros, P., Ottaviani, C., Arora, P., Pujol, V. C., Haunschild, D., Parlikad, A. K., Cetinkaya, O., Lutfiyya, H., Stankovski, V., Li, R., Ding, Y., Qadir, J., Abraham, A., Ghosh, S. K., Song, H. H., Sakellariou, R., Rana, O., & Rodrigues, J. J. P. C. (2024). Modern Computing: Vision and Challenges. *Telematics and Informatics Reports*, 13, 100116. https://www.sciencedirect.com/ science/article/pii/S2772503024000021

Guo, Y., Ganti, S., & Wu, Y. (2024). Enhancing Energy Efficiency in Telehealth Internet of Things Systems Through Fog and Cloud Computing Integration: Simulation Study. *JMIR Biomedical Engineering*, 9, e50175–e50175. https://doi .org/10.2196/50175

Hossain, D., Sultana, T., Akhter, S., Md. Imtiaz Hossain, Ngo Thien Thu, Luan, Lee, G.-W., & Huh, E.-N. (2023). The Role of Microservice Approach in Edge Computing: Opportunities, Challenges, and Research Directions. *ICT Express*. https://doi.org/10.1016/j.icte.2023.06.006

How Edge Computing Improves Data Processing Speed and Efficiency in Healthcare. (2024). https://binariks.com/blog/edge-computing-for-healthcare-data/

https://techcommunity.microsoft.com/t5/user/viewprofilepage/user-id/2477727. (2024). Revolutionizing Healthcare: The Impact of Cloud Computing and Artificial Intelligence. https://techcommunity.microsoft.com/t5/ai-ai-platform-blog /revolutionizing-healthcare-the-impact-of-cloud-computing-and/ba-p/4149668

Jeyaraman, N., Jeyaraman, M., Yadav, S., Ramasubramanian, S., Balaji, S., Muthu, S., P, C. L., Patro, B. P., Jeyaraman, N., Jeyaraman, M., Yadav, S., Ramasubramanian, S., Balaji, S., Muthu, S., P, C. L., & Patro, B. P. (2024). Applications of Fog Computing in Healthcare. *Cureus*, 16(7). https://doi.org/10.7759/cureus.64263

Lin, H. (2024). Ethical and Scalable Automation: A Governance and Compliance Framework for Business Applications. *arXiv preprint arXiv:2409.16872.*

Patan, L. (2024). Leveraging Cloud-Native Architecture for Scalable and Resilient Enterprise Applications: A Comprehensive Analysis. *International Journal of Computer Engineering and Technology (IJCET)*, 15(5), 583–591.

Rathi, V. K., Rajput, N. K., Mishra, S., Grover, B. A., Tiwari, P., Jaiswal, A. K., & Hossain, M. S. (2021). An Edge AI-Enabled IoT Healthcare Monitoring System for Smart Cities. *Computers & Electrical Engineering*, 96, 107524. https://doi.org /10.1016/j.compeleceng.2021.107524

Simon Barr. (2024). AI Scalability and Customization: How Can AI Fit in Your Healthcare. https://bhmpc.com/2024/09/ai-scalability-and-customization-how-ca n-ai-fit-in-your-healthcare-administration/

Verma, P., Gupta, A., Kumar, M., & Gill, S. S. (2023). FCMCPS-COVID: AI Propelled Fog-Cloud Inspired Scalable Medical Cyber-Physical System, Specific to Coronavirus Disease. *Internet of Things*, 23, 100828–100828. https://doi.org/10.1016/j.iot.2023.100828

Vultr Industry Cloud Solutions – Healthcare and Life Sciences - Vultr. (2024). https://www.vultr.com/solutions/healthcare-life-sciences/

Williams, E., Kienast, M., Medawar, E., Reinelt, J., Merola, A., Klopfenstein, S. A. I., Flint, A. R., Heeren, P., Poncette, A.-S., Balzer, F., Beimes, J., Bünau, P. von, Chromik, J., Arnrich, B., Scherf, N., & Niehaus, S. (2023). A Standardized Clinical Data Harmonization Pipeline for Scalable AI Application Deployment (FHIR-DHP): Validation and Usability Study. *JMIR Medical Informatics*, 11(1), e43847. https://doi.org/10.2196/43847

4 Big Data and AI Solutions for Transforming Healthcare

Frameworks, Challenges, and Future Directions

Houneida Sakly, Ramzi Guetari,
Naoufel Kraiem, and Mourad Abed

4.1 Introduction

4.1.1 Overview of Big Data and AI Integration in Healthcare

In the health care industry, the integration of Big Data and artificial intelligence (AI) is essential to improve patient outcomes, optimize operations, and improve the quality of care. Big Data simplifies the collection and analysis of in-depth patient health information, helps prevent epidemics, reduces costs, and improves treatment efficiency. Artificial intelligence technologies, such as machine learning and neural networks, are automating tasks for patients and health professionals, leading to more efficient procedures that drive innovation.

IBM's Watson Health and Flatiron Health have developed commercial platforms that use artificial intelligence for medical data analysis, enabling the analysis of medical data across hospitals and research institutions. These platforms help share medical data, advance cancer research, optimize risk assessment processes, and structure unstructured health data to gain meaningful insights.

There are many benefits to integrating Big Data into healthcare, as it allows researchers to access a large amount of patient information and thus enables pioneering medical discoveries. With the Internet of Things (IoT), healthcare professionals can more effectively monitor critical health indicators such as sleep patterns and heart rates. In addition, Big Data allows for personalized management tailored to high-risk patients while simplifying the overall health process. Ultimately, the combination of Big Data and artificial intelligence has the potential to transform patient management through accurate medicine and improved health outcomes. While data protection challenges remain, new technologies such as GPU accelerators and work schedules can improve hardware utilization and enhance artificial intelligence performance, ensuring robust data management. See references: (Dash et al., 2019) and (Singh, 2024).

DOI: 10.1201/9781003480594-4

Figure 4.1 Use of big data in healthcare (Singh, 2024).

4.1.2 *Prominence of Scalability in Healthcare Technologies*

Scalability is critical in healthcare technologies, especially with the integration of BigData and artificial intelligence. The health field generates large amounts of data from medical records, diagnostics, and IoT devices, which require efficient management and analysis to obtain relevant information. Expanding data pipelines and systems is critical for effectively managing these large databases.

In healthcare, Big Data is typically stored in data lakes that can accommodate different data formats and integrate with platforms such as relational databases or data warehouses. Tools such as Hadoop and Spark simplify the analysis of this raw data by distributing workloads across clustered environments as described in Figure 4.1. The cloud has gained popularity for large-scale systems because of its ability to be flexible and cost effective.

Advances in AI significantly improve data management procedures by providing advanced analytical skills. Through the alliance of Big Data and AI, healthcare companies can design personalized treatment plans, improve patient outcomes, and increase operational efficiency.

However, scalability poses challenges, especially with regard to data security and privacy compliance. With the exponential growth of medical data, it is becoming increasingly critical to adopt strong security measures and comply with privacy laws (Yang et al., 2021).

In the future, technologies such as blockchain offer secure methods for storing medical records, while new innovations promise improvements in patient management. By effectively addressing scalability challenges through the integration of big data and AI, healthcare organizations can discover new opportunities for innovation and improve patient outcomes. See references: (Dash et al., 2019) and (Mehta et al., 2019).

4.2   Role of Big Data in AI-driven Healthcare Innovations

4.2.1   *Applications of AI in Healthcare*

The health industry has undergone a major transformation due to artificial intelligence, particularly in the areas of detection and management. Artificial intelligence enables physicians to make accurate diagnoses and tailor treatments for patients. This advanced technology can predict the results of therapy and suggest the best actions based on factors such as medical history, genetics, lifestyle, and environmental influences. By analyzing large samples, artificial intelligence facilitates the identification of personalized therapies.

Artificial intelligence also plays a key role in drug discovery and development by analyzing complex data to uncover patterns that can lead to the creation of new drugs. This method increases the efficiency of research and accelerates the introduction of new drugs into the market.

In the field of radiology, artificial intelligence has significantly improved diagnostic accuracy when medical images are analyzed to detect subtle abnormalities that are often overlooked by the human eye. Using artificial intelligence assistants to highlight essential features in many images every day allows radiologists to improve both the quality and speed of their work.

Overall, the integration of AI in health optimizes decision-making processes and leads to personalized treatment plans that meet the specific needs of each patient. With continued advances in artificial intelligence, the healthcare industry, as described in Table 4.1 is moving toward greater efficiency and effectiveness in providing patient care. See reference: (Smith, 2023).

4.2.2   *Benefits of Combining Big Data with AI in Healthcare*

The integration of Big Data and artificial intelligence (AI) in healthcare has many benefits, such as changing patient management and the care landscape. By combining vast amounts of data with advanced artificial intelligence technologies, medical researchers have access to a wealth of information that has led to remarkable discoveries and breakthroughs.

One major advantage of this integration is the ability to provide personalized and accurate assistance. Given the availability of detailed patient data, healthcare professionals can tailor their treatments to meet the specific needs of each patient, resulting in improved patient outcomes and service quality. This personalized approach improves both patient experiences and facilitates the delivery of medical care by providing timely, personalized treatment to high-risk patients.

In addition, the combination of Big Data and artificial intelligence allows for continuous monitoring of various health data through technologies such as the Internet of Things. This allows vital signs, lifestyle patterns, and other health-related information to be tracked, which supports early detection of disease and improves management strategies.

Table 4.1 List of some large companies that provide services for big data analysis in the healthcare sector

Company	Description
IBM Watson Health[1]	Provides the exchange of clinical and health-related data across hospitals, researchers, and providers for advanced research purposes.
MedeAnalytics[2]	Offers performance management solutions, health systems and programs, and health analytics, complemented by an extensive history of patient data management.
Health Fidelity[3]	Offers a management solution for risk assessment in healthcare organization workflows, along with strategies for optimization and correction.
Roam Analytics[4]	Offers systems for analyzing extensive unstructured healthcare data to get valuable insights.
Flatiron Health[5]	Offers applications for the organization and enhancement of oncology data to optimize cancer treatment.
Enlitic[6]	Provides deep learning utilizing extensive datasets from clinical assessments for healthcare diagnostics.
Digital Reasoning Systems[7]	Offers cognitive computing services and data analytics solutions for the processing and organization of unstructured data into relevant information.
Ayasdi[8]	Offers an AI-enhanced platform for clinical variability, population health, risk management, and various healthcare analytics.
Linguamatics[9]	Offers a text mining tool for extracting significant information from unstructured healthcare data.
Apixio[10]	Offers a cognitive computing platform for the analysis of clinical data and PDF health records to produce comprehensive insights.
Roam Analytics[11]	Delivers natural language processing infrastructure for contemporary healthcare systems
Lumiata[12]	provides analytics and risk management services to optimize outcomes in healthcare.
OptumHealth[13]	Provides healthcare analytics, enhances contemporary health system infrastructure, and offers comprehensive and creative solutions for the healthcare sector.

(Dash et al., 2023)
[1] https://www.ibm.com/watson/health/index-1.html
[2] https://medeanalytics.com/
[3] https://healthfidelity.com/
[4] https://roamanalytics.com/
[5] https://flatiron.com/
[6] https://www.enlitic.com/
[7] https://digitalreasoning.com/
[8] https://www.ayasdi.com/
[9] https://www.linguamatics.com/
[10] https://www.apixio.com/
[11] https://roamanalytics.com/
[12] https://www.lumiata.com
[13] https://www.optum.com/

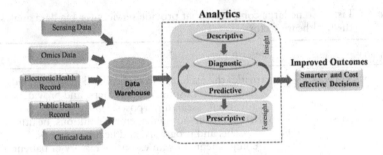

Figure 4.2 Big Data analytics workflow: Data from various sources are processed to enable smarter, affordable healthcare (Dash et al., 2019).

In addition, combining Big Data with artificial intelligence, as seen in Figure 4.2, enhances the efficiency of data management procedures. Innovations based on artificial intelligence optimize data management and improve decision-making capabilities and costs while fostering data-driven medical practices.

In summary, the combination of Big Data and AI in health offers many benefits, such as improved health outcomes, simplified procedures, improved data management, and customized processing methods. This progress has the potential to transform the healthcare sector as is currently known. See references: (Singh, 2024) and (Smith, 2023).

4.3 Building Scalable Data Pipelines

4.3.1 Definitions and Importance of Data Pipelines

The crucial role of data pipelines is to integrate Big Data and artificial intelligence into healthcare. They involve a series of processes that collect, transform, and send data for use in artificial intelligence applications, ensuring efficient flow of information from different sources, standardizing data, and making it compatible with artificial intelligence algorithms.

In the healthcare sector, these channels are essential for managing the large amounts of medical data generated every day. Using technologies such as GPUs and artificial intelligence accelerators, data pipelines can efficiently process complex datasets and generate valuable insights. With automation tools such as Argo, tasks can be seamlessly completed within these pipelines, making it easy to integrate and manage AI-based workflows.

The key elements of scalable data pipelines include federal data lakes, warehouses, and databases, which enable healthcare institutions to efficiently store and analyze large amounts of data, whether or not they are structured. Using these technologies, healthcare providers can optimize data management procedures and improve patient outcomes.

In summary, data pipelines, as described in Figure 4.3, play a key role in integrating Big Data and artificial intelligence into the healthcare field,

Figure 4.3 Diagram of data flow from sources (data warehouse, SaaS, mainframe) to data lake creation (delivery, refinement, catalog) and then to managed platforms such as AWS and Azure

Source: Reference (What is Data Integration? Definition, Examples and Use Cases, 2024).

enabling the flow of information to artificial intelligence applications and supporting advanced analytics for better patient management. As new technologies such as blockchain emerge to protect medical data, future trends suggest a continued focus on improving scalability and efficiency in healthcare through the integration of big data and artificial intelligence solutions. See references: (Leppitsch & Fatima, 2023), (Smith, 2023), and (Thantilage et al., 2023).

4.3.2 Technologies Supporting Scalable Data Pipelines

Automation tools are critical in building scalable data pipelines for the AI-driven healthcare industry. The essential role of workflow schedulers such as Argo is to automate task execution, manage dependencies, and resolve issues in data workflows. Argo helps design complex, data-rich workflows by offering features such as parallelism, conditional execution, and error management. By using these automation tools, healthcare organizations can streamline their Big Data processing tasks, improving the coordination and management of AI workloads. In addition to workflow schedulers, real-time processing frameworks are essential to support resilient data pipelines in the healthcare field. This structure facilitates the efficient management of large volumes of medical data, leading to better adaptation of data and analysis in real time. Apache Spark and Hadoop are frequently used in addition to automated tools to optimize data management procedures in healthcare environments. This combination enables companies to strengthen their data management skills and ensure scalability when faced with large amounts of medical data. Overall, the integration of automation tools with real-time processing frameworks significantly improves scalable data pipelines in AI-based healthcare innovations. These technologies enable healthcare institutions to manage large amounts of data efficiently, process information quickly, and extract valuable insights from complex datasets, resulting in improved patient management outcomes. See references: (Dash et al., 2019), (Smith, 2023), and (Presley, 2024).

4.4   Data Lakes, Warehouses, and Federated Databases

4.4.1   *Understanding Data lakes, Warehouses, and Federated Databases*

Effectively managing medical data requires a thorough understanding of federal data lakes, warehouses, and databases. Data lakes function as centralized repositories for raw, unprocessed data, enabling real-time search capabilities without relying on complex ETL (Extract, Transform, Load) processes. In contrast, data warehouses offer a structured and cohesive framework that facilitates seamless data retrieval from administrative and biological systems.

Datamarts focus on extracting and organizing specific subsets of raw data, supporting targeted analyses, while functional data is systematically arranged into tables to simplify data creation and utilization. A critical aspect of this ecosystem is the data reuse pipeline, which relies on key components such as Electronic Health Records (EHR) to serve as primary data sources and ETL processes to transform and integrate the data for downstream use, as described in Figure 4.4. These components enable efficient data reuse, promoting better integration and accessibility of vital medical information.

The study of various types of medical data highlights the importance of security and confidentiality, particularly with respect to structured, semistructured, and unstructured data in medical environments. Structured content is easily organized but not flexible, whereas unstructured content, although difficult to manage, contains valuable information. The semistructured data merge the characteristics of both, making it an ideal choice for medical data storage as depicted in Table 4.2 and Table 4.3.

A centralized architecture for medical data storage (see Figure 4.5) is recommended for its advantages in confidentiality, scalability, and traceability. By consolidating data in a single, secure location, it simplifies access control and auditing, making it easier to monitor compliance and ensure data privacy. In contrast, a distributed architecture offers benefits in terms of resilience and scalability, as it disperses data across multiple locations, reducing the risk of a single point of failure and enhancing fault tolerance. Each approach has unique strengths, and the choice between them depends

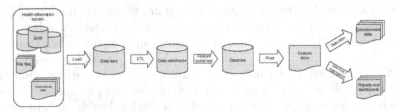

Figure 4.4 Components of the data reuse pipeline: EHR (electronic health records) and ETL (extract-transform-load) (Lamer et al., 2024).

Table 4.2 Characteristics of each component of the data reuse pipeline

Characteristics	Software	Data lake	Data warehouse	Datamarts	Feature store
Content	Data and metadata	Data and metadata	Data	Features	Features and metadata about feature
Architecture	Distributed	Centralized	Centralized	Centralized	Centralized
Detail level	Fine-grained	Fine-grained	Fine-grained	Aggregated	Aggregated
Data	Raw	Raw	Cleaned	Cleaned	Cleaned
Nomenclature	Heterogeneous	Heterogeneous	Standardized	Standardized	Standardized
Data model	Normalized	Normalized	Normalized	Normalized	Denormalized
Data structure	Row-oriented	Row-oriented	Row-oriented	Row-oriented	Column-oriented
Purpose	Transactional software purpose	Ad hoc exploratory queries	All purposes	Prespecified purpose	Prespecified purpose

(Lamer et al., 2024)

Table 4.3 Advantages and disadvantages of the components of the data reuse pipeline

Component	Advantages	Disadvantages
Data lake	• All data sources on the same server • Autonomy from source software • Real-time query processing and data analysis without the necessity for a fully developed extract-transform-load (ETL) process	• Inconsistencies in data formats and structures • The absence of a standardized schema can complicate queries. • Analyses reproducibility
Data warehouse	• The unified data model facilitates querying data from both administrative and biological systems by linking data from both systems and ensuring uniform model conventions. • Relevant data are preserved at the highest level of granularity (e.g., dates, diagnoses, and all biological parameters), facilitating the resolution of various inquiries without the necessity of prior identification.	• ETL process must be implemented to standardize the data • Multidimensional data model with several statistical units • Fine-grained data is not directly usable and adapted for statistical analysis or decision-making
Datamarts	• Features are ready to be used directly	• Features remain structured in a row format (i.e., one feature per row) across several datamarts.
Feature store	• Employing features directly, eliminating the necessity for data management operations such as merging datamarts or restructuring features into columns.	• Having developed the entire pipeline beforehand

(Lamer et al., 2024)

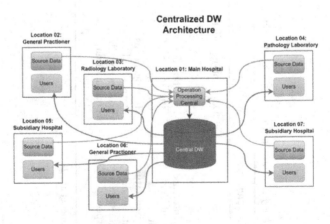

Figure 4.5 Centralized architecture (Thantilage et al., 2023).

Table 4.4 Radiotherapy research data types within their common IT systems

Information type	Data examples	IT healthcare system
Baseline clinical data	Demographics (including comorbidity and family history), TNM-stage, date of diagnosis, histopathology	HIS, TDS
Diagnostic imaging data	Diagnostic CT, MR, and PET imaging	PACS
Radiotherapy treatment planning data	Delineation/structure sets, planning-CT, dose matrix, beam setup, prescribed dose and fractions	PACS, RIS
Radiotherapy treatment delivery data	Cone beam CTs, orthogonal EPID imaging, delivered fractions	PACS, RIS
Nonradiotherapy treatment data	Surgery, chemotherapy	HIS, TDS
Outcome data	Survival, local control, distant failure, toxicity (including patient-reported outcomes), quality of life	EDC, TDS
Follow-up imaging data	Follow-up CT, MR and PET imaging	PACS
Biological data	Sample storage, shipping, tracing and lab results	LIMS
Additional study conduct data	Study design, protocol, eligibility criteria	EDC, CTMS

(Skripcak et al., 2014)

on the healthcare organization's specific requirements for data accessibility, security, and system robustness.

In the field of radiation therapy, as described Table 4.4, federal databases are essential for providing comprehensive data for analysis. This method allows for the storage of various types of radiotherapy research data in common computer systems such as HERs, HISs, PACSs, RISs, EDCs, and TDSs, thus ensuring efficient searches of different sources of information to support complex analyses, as shown in Figure 4.4 and Table 4.5. Ultimately, understanding the complexities of federal data lakes, warehouses and databases is critical to leveraging big data and artificial intelligence in healthcare. By taking into account privacy and scalability issues, healthcare companies can improve their data management processes and drive innovation in patient care. See references: (Thantilage et al., 2023), (Lamer et al., 2024), and (Skripcak et al., 2014).

4.4.2 Advantages and Challenges of Each Approach

Data lakes act as centralized storage systems for raw and unprocessed data, accommodating different formats and supporting big data analytics, machine learning, and smart functionality. While data warehouses store processed data for specific applications, data lakes offer great flexibility, making them invaluable in various sectors such as commerce, finance, and events.

Table 4.5 Examples of electronic healthcare records (EHRs), also known as electronic healthcare modules, with their uses

EHR/Module	Deployment
Patient administration system (PAS)	Patient registration, referral receipt, appointment scheduling, and hospital bed load management; frequently linked to a bed management module that evaluates bed status and facilitates bed state assessment.
Infection management EHR	Analysis of the spread of infections
Labs EHR (pathology virology and microbiology), also known as a laboratory information system (LIM)	Oversight of sample progression within the laboratory procedure; samples are analyzed and results are uploaded.
Radiology picture archive and communication system (PACS)	Vendor-neutral archive systems which store the images and the clinical information on the scan
Radiology information system (RIS)	Coordination of radiology appointments and radiographer/sonographer operations, documentation of scan type and dosage parameters; integration with radiology PACS.
Community EHR	Out of hospital scheduling, offline access to medical records, documentation of patient information during home visits
Theatre systems	Schedule patients, record theatre notes, and allows for monitoring of theater equipment
Emergency department system	Registering patients; often there are links to clinical modules to allow requesting
Order communication (order comms)	Frequently utilized for requisitioning diagnostic assessments, such as blood tests necessitating labeling and printing; it is commonly associated with the results module.
Results EHR	Summary of diagnostic test outcomes, encompassing both laboratory results and non-laboratory findings (e.g., radiological assessments, physiological evaluations).
Observation EHR	Recording vital signs
Prescribing and drug management EHR	Prescribing, dispensing and inventory management purposes, as well as financial management of inventory
Documentation/clinical notes EHR	Documenting of clinical information inside and outside of clinical specialities
Maternal EHR	Management of maternal and fetal care during prenatal and postnatal periods, encompassing documentation and reporting. Upon the birth of the infant, this module assigns an NHS number that remains with the individual for their lifetime.
Child health EHR	Vaccinations, growth charts, and other algorithms and forms related to child health
Single sign on	Use of biometrics (e.g., face recognition or fingerprints) or smart cards (akin to personalized bank cards) to facilitate the login of clinical users across several heterogeneous IT systems, therefore obviating the need for users to recall multiple passwords.

(Idowu et al., 2023)

Data warehouses, on the other hand, play a key role in healthcare for structured data analysis. They gather the historical data needed to obtain information that improves the delivery of healthcare. By preserving detailed information such as dates and diagnostics, these warehouses allow for comprehensive analyses without the need for predefined questions. However, there are difficulties in standardizing the ETL (extract, transform, load) process needed to convert raw data into practical insights.

Federal databases provide a decentralized method for managing medical data across multiple healthcare sites. With this system, each locality can manage its own data while allowing for modular evolution, faster responses, greater reliability, and improved performance. Federal databases effectively address the complexities of medical data storage, such as confidentiality, scalability, and traceability, which are essential in healthcare settings. In summary, while data lakes are distinguished by their ability to store various raw data for extensive use, data warehouses specialize in the structured analysis of health-critical data. Federal databases are an effective solution for managing distributed medical data, balancing local management with the importance of integrated insights. See references: ("What is a Data Lake? Data lake vs. Warehouse" | Microsoft Azure, 2024) and (Thantilage et al., 2023).

4.5 Utilization of AI-driven Innovations for Efficient Data Management

4.5.1 Role of AI in Optimizing Data Management Processes

Artificial intelligence (AI) plays an important role in simplifying data management methods in the healthcare sector by automating tasks that are usually performed by humans. An example of this is AutoML, which automates machine learning processes, making it easier to analyze and manipulate large datasets. By integrating AutoML, healthcare professionals can improve the efficiency of data management procedures, save time, and reduce potential errors.

In addition, natural language processing (NLP) stands out as another key technology that enhances data management in healthcare environments. NLP allows the analysis of texts and the retrieval of information from unstructured data sources such as medical notes or patient records. This method enables caregivers to extract valuable information from large amounts of textual data in a fast and accurate manner.

The contribution of artificial intelligence technologies, such as AutoML and NLP, to data management is changing the way healthcare organizations manage their data, as shown in Figure 4.6. Using these tools, healthcare professionals can simplify data management, improve decision-making processes, and ultimately improve patient outcomes. See references: (Dash et al., 2019) and (Idowu et al., 2023).

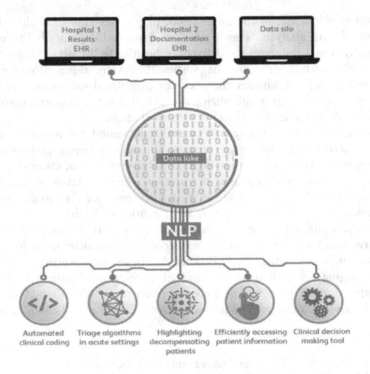

Figure 4.6 Data sorting uses the open-source CogStack framework to create a data lake. NLP cleans data and extracts useful information from EHR (electronic health records) (Idowu et al., 2023).

4.6   Data Security and Privacy Concerns in Big Data and AI Integration

4.6.1   *Importance of Security Measures in Healthcare Data Management*

Ensuring the security and confidentiality of medical data is crucial to preserving the integrity of patient information. With the increase in medical data, preserving sensitive medical records has become a top priority. The EU's GDPR recognizes health and genetic data as "sensitive information", highlighting the importance of strong security measures.

Multiple levels of security, such as access controls, encryption, and audit trails, are required to prevent unauthorized access and maintain patient confidentiality. Techniques such as data detection and manipulation are essential to preserve the integrity of the data while allowing meaningful analysis. It is essential to comply with regulations such as HIPAA and GDPR to avoid legal consequences, which makes it essential to implement comprehensive data management policies that define attributions, access rights, usage rules, and safeguards.

Given the complexity of medical data sources, it is essential to have key data storage capacity. Scalable architectures allow for efficient processing of different datasets while ensuring traceability for accurate interpretation of medical data. Using secure storage methods through distributed file systems, reliable solutions can be found to handle large volumes of medical data.

In summary, it is essential to incorporate strong security measures into medical data management to protect patient privacy, meet regulatory standards, and improve overall data security in medical environments. Adopting a multidimensional approach is essential for effectively addressing the complexities of medical data while fostering trust and security in patient care. This strategy integrates technological, ethical, and regulatory considerations, enabling healthcare systems to navigate the diverse challenges associated with managing medical data in AI-driven environments. Emphasizing transparency, data protection, and compliance with regulatory standards ensures that AI systems remain not only efficient but also aligned with patient privacy and ethical principles. This approach creates a trusted environment where patients feel secure about the handling of their data, and healthcare providers can confidently apply advanced technologies to increase diagnostic accuracy, personalize treatments, and improve the overall quality of care. This fosters stronger trust between patients and providers, paving the way for a more responsible and impactful adoption of AI in healthcare as recommended in Table 4.6. (Thantilage et al., 2023).

4.6.2 Privacy Regulations Compliance

It is crucial to respect confidentiality rules to ensure the security of medical data within data storage systems. With the increasing complexity of medical data, maintaining patient privacy standards is increasingly crucial. The General Data Protection Regulation (GDPR) in Europe defines health and genetic information as sensitive and requires strict safeguards. Compliance with regulations such as GDPR, HIPAA, and local laws is essential to avoid legal issues and maintain patient confidence. Deidentification techniques, such as data masking, can preserve patient privacy while allowing valuable analysis of medical data. It is essential to adopt key security measures, such as access controls, encryption and audits, to prevent unauthorized access and reduce cyber threats. Effective data management practices are also essential for defining data ownership, access permissions, and protection protocols. To deliver medical data into data storage systems, a flexible infrastructure that can handle large amounts of data without compromising performance is needed. Installing a consent management system can ensure the security of data sharing, especially in emergency situations. After complying with confidentiality rules and adopting best practices, healthcare companies can protect patient data while benefiting from the insights of big data analytics. See reference (Thantilage et al., 2023).

Table 4.6 Clinical DW observations and recommendations

Features and challenges	Observations and recommendations
Data standardization	Standardizing data is essential for maintaining consistency and accuracy across all data sources. A standardized data model and data dictionary for the data warehouse would guarantee that all data conforms to these specifications.
Privacy preservation	Protecting patient confidentiality is essential in any clinical data warehouse. This entails using deidentification methods, such as masking, to protect patient data while facilitating substantive analysis.
Data security	The security of the data warehouse is paramount. This entails the implementation of robust access restrictions, encryption, and additional security measures to avert unauthorized access and protect against cyber dangers.
Compliance	Clinical data warehouses must adhere to multiple data protection requirements, including GDPR, HIPAA, and CCPA, among others. Organizations must verify that their data warehouse architecture and procedures adhere to these regulations to prevent potential legal complications.
Data governance	Specify the ownership of the data, the individuals authorized to access it, the permissible uses, and the required protective measures. An explicit data governance approach guarantees that all stakeholders comprehend the protocols and legislation pertaining to data security and privacy.
Data distribution	The distribution of data is a critical factor in clinical data warehousing, necessitating the design of a system capable of managing substantial data quantities while ensuring optimal performance. A distributed file system offers a scalable and fault-tolerant method for storing and processing substantial data quantities.
Data sharing	The sharing of data inside clinical data warehouse architecture presents complexities related to privacy and security considerations. Establish a consent management system that empowers patients to regulate the sharing of their data and designate recipients. Furthermore, facilitate safe data sharing for emergency care centers to obtain patient records during crucial situations.

(Thantilage et al., 2023)

4.7 Future Trends in the Integration of Big Data and AI Scalability in Healthcare

4.7.1 Advancements Such As Blockchain Technology for Secure Health Records

Revolutionary technologies, especially blockchain, are transforming the secure management of health records. As medical data becomes increasingly digital and connected to advanced Big Data and artificial intelligence solutions, there is an increasing need for strong security measures. The decentralized and immutable file system of the blockchain has a major advantage in preserving patient confidentiality and record integrity.

By implementing blockchain in the healthcare sector, we can create a secure network where patient data is encrypted, recorded, and distributed across multiple parties. With this architecture, no entity can control the entire database, which significantly reduces the risk of data breaches or unauthorized access. In addition, blockchain technology provides transparent audits, allowing healthcare providers to track and verify any changes made to medical records.

The use of technology promotes seamless interoperability between different healthcare providers while maintaining strict confidentiality standards. Smart contracts can be used to define permissions for specific patient information, ensuring compliance with regulations such as HIPAA and GDPR. This concentration of control strengthens trust between the relevant actors and promotes cooperation in providing high-quality medical care.

In the future, advances in blockchain technology are expected to further enhance healthcare data security and confidentiality. Advances such as evidence of nonknowledge and homomorphic encryption provide additional protection for sensitive medical information. As the digital transformation of the healthcare sector continues, blockchain integration will be critical to protecting patient data and optimizing care delivery procedures. See reference: (Babar et al., 2024).

4.7.2   Emerging Technologies for Enhanced Patient Care

Cutting-edge technology is transforming patient management in healthcare, with federated learning (FL) as a major innovation. FL is a machine learning

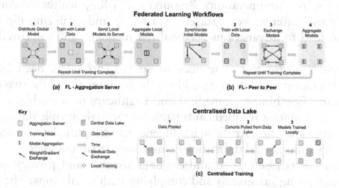

Figure 4.7 Federated learning (FL) workflows differ from centralized data lake training. In the FL aggregation server model, training nodes submit partially trained models to a central server for aggregation. The FL peer-to-peer approach involves nodes exchanging models and performing local aggregation. In contrast, Centralized Training sees data sources contributing to a central data lake for local, independent training (Rieke et al., 2020).

method that allows multiple companies to analyze large datasets together while preserving patient privacy. By combining internal and external data sources, FL facilitates the creation of advanced predictive models that increase the accuracy of patient outcome predictions and improve medical management. In addition, advances in Big Data analytics enable healthcare providers to gain valuable insights from large data collections. Together, FL and Big Data analytics play critical roles in transitioning healthcare in the digital age, improving patient outcomes, preserving privacy, and simplifying care delivery procedures. Using FL in medical data analysis is critical due to the sensitive nature of patient information, which requires strict compliance with data protection regulations such as HIPAA and GDPR. FL allows healthcare institutions to work together on data analysis without compromising the privacy or security of individuals. In addition, the combination of FL and big data analysis has yielded promising results in reducing operating costs and improving the efficiency of healthcare systems. Research shows that billions of dollars can be saved each year in the healthcare sector by integrating these technologies and optimizing operating procedures. In short, technologies such as federated learning and Big Data analytics have considerable potential to improve patient care. By adopting these innovations, healthcare providers can obtain critical information from large databases while prioritizing patient privacy and regulatory standards. See reference: (Babar et al., 2024).

4.8 Conclusion

The integration of Big Data and artificial intelligence (AI) in the healthcare field has considerable potential to transform patient management and medical knowledge. Using data harmonization tools that meet standards such as Fast Healthcare Interoperability Resources (FHIRs), healthcare companies can easily use different key datasets. Mastering and analyzing Big Data in depth can lead to advances in personalized medicine and improved health services.

As digital information continues to spread, providers need access to advanced computing solutions to address the complexities of the massive volume of data. Combining biomedical and healthcare data enables organizations to create innovative medical treatments through flexible data pipelines and advanced analytics. Artificial intelligence can simplify data management, optimize operations, and dramatically improve patient outcomes.

However, it is essential to address data security and privacy issues by establishing strong safeguards and complying with regulations. The upcoming trends in health synergy between Big Data and AI include advances such as blockchain technology for medical record security and innovative solutions to improve patient management. Overall, collaboration between Big Data and AI has the potential to transform the healthcare landscape by connecting people and improving the quality of patient care. By using flexible data infrastructures, advanced analytical techniques, and secure technologies, healthcare institutions are able to foster innovation and provide personalized and effective assistance. See references: (Dash et al., 2019), (Batko & Ślęzak, 2022), and (Williams et al., 2023).

References

Babar, M., Qureshi, B., & Anis Koubaa. (2024). Review on federated learning for digital transformation in healthcare through big data analytics. *Future Generation Computer Systems*, 160, 14–28. https://doi.org/10.1016/j.future.2024.05.046

Batko, K., & Ślęzak, A. (2022). The use of big data analytics in healthcare. *Journal of Big Data*, 9(1). https://www.ncbi.nlm.nih.gov/pmc/articles/PMC8733917/

Dash, S., Shakyawar, S. K., Sharma, M., & Kaushik, S. (2019). Big data in healthcare: Management, analysis and future prospects. *Journal of Big Data*, 6(1), 1–25. https://doi.org/10.1186/s40537-019-0217-0

Idowu, E. A. A., Teo, J., Salih, S., Valverde, J., & Yeung, J. A. (2023). Streams, rivers and data lakes: An introduction to understanding modern electronic healthcare records. *Clinical Medicine*, 23(4), 409. https://doi.org/10.7861/clinmed.2022-0325

Smith, J. (2023). Big Data in Healthcare: Revolutionizing Patient Care with AI. https://greenplum.org/big-data-in-healthcare-revolutionizing-patient-care-with-ai/

Lamer, A., Chloé Saint-Dizier, Paris, N., & Chazard, E. (2024). Data lake, data warehouse, datamart, and feature store: Their contributions to the complete data reuse pipeline. *JMIR Medical Informatics*, 12, e54590–e54590. https://doi.org/10.2196/54590

Mehta, N., Pandit, A., & Shukla, S. (2019). Transforming healthcare with big data analytics and artificial intelligence: A systematic mapping study. *Journal of Biomedical Informatics*, 100, 103311. https://doi.org/10.1016/j.jbi.2019.103311

Leppitsch, M., & Fatima, S. (2023). Mastering Healthcare Data Pipelines: A Comprehensive Guide from Biome Analytics. https://www.ascend.io/blog/mastering-healthcare-data-pipelines-a-comprehensive-guide-from-biome-analytics/

Molly Presley. (2024). Cutting-Edge Infrastructure Best Practices for Enterprise AI Data Pipelines. https://www.bigdatawire.com/2024/07/23/cutting-edge-infrastructure-best-practices-for-enterprise-ai-data-pipelines/

Rieke, N., Hancox, J., Li, W., Milletarì, F., Roth, H. R., Albarqouni, S., Bakas, S., Galtier, M. N., Landman, B. A., Maier-Hein, K., Ourselin, S., Sheller, M., Summers, R. M., Trask, A., Xu, D., Baust, M., & Cardoso, M. J. (2020). The future of digital health with federated learning. *NPJ Digital Medicine*, 3(1), 1–7. https://doi.org/10.1038/s41746-020-00323-1

Singh, C. (2024). The Role of Big Data and AI in Healthcare. https://www.appventurez.com/blog/big-data-ai-healthcare-sector

Skripcak, T., Belka, C., Bosch, W., Brink, C., Brunner, T., Budach, V., Büttner, D., Debus, J., Dekker, A., Grau, C., Gulliford, S., Hurkmans, C., Just, U., Krause, M., Lambin, P., Langendijk, J. A., Lewensohn, R., Lühr, A., Maingon, P., & Masucci, M. (2014). Creating a data exchange strategy for radiotherapy research: Toward federated databases and anonymised public datasets. *Radiotherapy and Oncology*, 113(3), 303–309. https://doi.org/10.1016/j.radonc.2014.10.001

Thantilage, R. D., Le-Khac, N.-A., & Kechadi, M-Tahar. (2023). Healthcare data security and privacy in Data Warehouse architectures. *Informatics in Medicine Unlocked*, 39, 101270. https://doi.org/10.1016/j.imu.2023.101270

What is a Data Lake? Data Lake vs. Warehouse | Microsoft Azure. (2024). https://azure.microsoft.com/en-us/resources/cloud-computing-dictionary/what-is-a-data-lake

What is Data Integration? Definition, Examples & Use Cases. (2024). https://www.qlik.com/us/data-integration

Williams, E., Kienast, M., Medawar, E., Reinelt, J., Merola, A., Klopfenstein, S. A. I., Flint, A. R., Heeren, P., Poncette, A.-S., Balzer, F., Beimes, J., Bünau, P. von, Chromik, J., Arnrich, B., Scherf, N., & Niehaus, S. (2023). A standardized clinical data harmonization pipeline for scalable AI application deployment (FHIR-DHP): Validation and usability study. *JMIR Medical Informatics*, 11(1), e43847. https://doi.org/10.2196/43847

Yang, Y. C., Islam, S. U., Noor, A., Khan, S., Afsar, W., & Nazir, S. (2021). Influential usage of big data and artificial intelligence in healthcare. *Computational & Mathematical Methods in Medicine*, 2021, 1–13. https://doi.org/10.1155/2021/5812499

5 Scalable Machine Learning for Healthcare
Techniques, Applications, and Collaborative Frameworks

Alaa Eddinne ben Hmida, Houneida Sakly, Ramzi Guetari, and Naoufel Kraiem

5.1 Introduction

5.1.1 Overview of Machine Learning in Healthcare

Machine learning has made great strides in healthcare, including models in key environments. The focus is now on the proper exploitation of key clinical data and adaptation to natural variations that can impact model performance. Key open data such as BRATS, ADNI, and NIH PLCO played a critical role in this breakthrough. Deep learning models present a great opportunity for healthcare applications, including predicting mortality rates and estimating patient stay times. Evaluation studies based on the MIMIC-III dataset show that deep learning models are consistently superior to traditional machine learning methods and gravity scoring systems. They are skilled in raw data management, effectively appropriating complex representations from different data sources (Alzubaidi et al., 2021).

In addition, network learning has proven to be an effective strategy for building machine learning models with varied data from different regions. The performance of these federal models improves when more patients participate in the central analysis, highlighting the benefits of collaboration in medical analysis. Large healthcare facilities can also benefit from being included in federal learning networks. This highlights the importance of scalability and collaborative data analysis in improving health outcomes. See the following references: (Purushotham et al., 2018), (Liu et al., 2022), and (Zhang et al., 2022).

5.1.2 Scaling Models in Healthcare Applications

It is increasingly critical to improve machine learning models in the healthcare field as the sector has turned to model implementation. This transition poses challenges related to data management, requiring effective solutions to provide key clinical data to ensure accurate and precise predictions in time. Robust data preprocessing techniques are essential for managing large medical datasets. Advanced methods such as deep generative models, federated

DOI: 10.1201/9781003480594-5

learning models, and transformational models have demonstrated their potential to extend datasets and improve model performance.

Furthermore, it is essential to monitor and respond to natural fluctuations in data that can negatively impact the accuracy of the model when it is integrated into medical environments. Identifying these changes helps maintain the reliability of machine learning models, which preserves their effectiveness in real applications, as described in Table 5.1.

In summary, the flexibility of machine learning models has a significant effect on clinical outcomes and patient management standards. By solving data challenges, using effective preprocessing methods, and leveraging innovative approaches such as federated learning, the healthcare sector can fully exploit the benefits of large-scale machine learning models to achieve better patient outcomes, as described in AI and ML technologies in pharmaceutical and clinical research as an example. See reference: (Zhang et al., 2022).

5.2 Training Machine Learning Models on Large Datasets

5.2.1 Data Preprocessing for Large Healthcare Datasets

Preprocessing data is crucial to ensure the effectiveness and accuracy of machine learning models, especially when working with extensive medical data such as MIMIC-III, which contains detailed clinical information from ICU patients. A key part of this procedure is to resolve the non-data points, exceptions, and ambiguous information frequently found in historical medical records, as these discrepancies can have a negative impact on model performance. Good hygiene and preprocessing are essential to obtain accurate predictions and insights.

It is essential to select the characteristics relevant for model formation. MIMIC-III includes many clinical variables, such as heart rate, blood pressure, and laboratory results, which require careful manipulation and selection to improve model performance. Using feature engineering techniques, valuable information can be obtained from these variables, which improves the prediction capabilities of machine learning models.

Standardization and scaling also play crucial roles in preparing data for large medical datasets. The standardization of numerical characteristics and their adaptation to a wide range reduce biases during model formation and promote convergence in optimization procedures. This allows machine learning models to effectively recognize patterns in data without being influenced by different dimensions.

In short, effective data preprocessing methods, such as MIMIC-III, are essential when dealing with large medical datasets. By methodically addressing issues such as missing values, exceptions, feature selection, normalization, and growth, researchers can ensure that machine learning models produce reliable and accurate results. See references: (Sarker, 2021) and (Purushotham et al., 2018).

Table 5.1 Literature of companies using AI and ML technologies in pharmaceutical and clinical research

Field	Technology and outcome	Industry and collaborations
Drug design	Novel therapeutic antibodies	Exscientia
Molecular drug discovery	AtomNet — a deep learning-based computational framework for structure-oriented drug creation	AtomWise
Gene mutation related disease	Recursion operating system utilizing machine learning for biological and chemical datasets	Recursion
Drug design	Ligand- and structure-based de novo drug design, especially in multiparametric optimization	Iktos
Drug discovery	Generative modeling AI technology	Iktos and Galapagos
Drug development	Potential preclinical candidates	Iktos and Ono Pharma
Drug design	Rapid drug design by software "Makya"	Iktos and Sygnature Discovery
Drug discovery and drug development	Pharma.AI, PandaMics, ALS.AI	Insilico Medicine
Drug target and drug development	ChatPandaGPT	Insilico Medicine
Drug development	The mobility of proteins in drug development is significant. RLY-4008: A novel allosteric inhibitor that is panmutant and isoform selective for PI3Kα.	Relay therapeutics
Drug discovery	AI and machine learning for selection of drug target	BenevolentAI
Drug target	Drug target selection for chronic kidney disease and idiopathic pulmonary fibrosis	BenevolentAI and AstraZeneca, GlaxoSmithKline, Pfizer
Clinical trials	AI in clinical trials	Pfizer and Vysioneer
Disease treatment	AI and supercomputing for oral COVID-19 treatment Paxloid	Pfizer
Drug discovery	NASH drugs and sequencing behemoth Illumina	AstraZeneca and Viking therapeutics
Drug development	Trials360.ai platform in clinical trials for site feasibility, site engagement and patient recruitment	Janssen
Drug research	Automate the review of medical literature by the application of natural language processing.	Sanofi
Drug development	AI in drug development	BioMed X and Sanofi
Drug research and drug development	AI empowerment and AI exploration platforms	Novartis and Microsoft
Drug discovery	AI drug discovery platform	Bayer

(Vora et al., 2023)

5.2.2   Techniques for Efficient Model Training on Large Datasets

Machine learning models can be optimized across many health datasets via different strategies. An effective method is to use pretrained language models, such as DeBERTa with 1.5 trillion parameters and GPT-3 with 175 trillion parameters, which are designed to efficiently process large amounts of data, as described in Table 5.2. and Table 5.3. They use parallel processing and model parallelism methods to manage large datasets efficiently. In addition, the combination of precision drive and gradient build-up reduces memory use and improves drive speed.

Another valuable strategy is to leverage distributed and parallel processing frameworks such as PyTorch and TensorFlow, allowing for distributed training across multiple nodes. This accelerates model convergence and improves scalability. In addition, learning transfer techniques allows for the refinement of pretrained models for specific medical tasks, which improves training effectiveness on large datasets.

In summary, it is essential to use advanced techniques such as prelanguage model training, distributed processing frameworks, and transfer learning methods for the effective training of machine learning models in the healthcare field. This strategy improves both the scalability and overall efficiency of machine learning applications in the healthcare sector. See references: ("Gcore Named a Leader in 2024 GigaOm Radar for Edge Development Platforms", 2024) and (Wang et al., 2022).

5.3   Distributed and Parallel Processing Frameworks

5.3.1   Introduction to Distributed Computing in Healthcare

The introduction of distributed computing in healthcare has revolutionized the capacity and effectiveness of machine learning models. This approach uses multiple interconnected computers to manage and analyze large datasets that exceed the capacity of any single machine. By enabling horizontal growth, distributed computing enhances hardware training capabilities, thus allowing for the efficient management of large amounts of data.

Each machine in a distributed system participates in the formation of model segments or data subsets, resulting in faster processing times than those of single-machine configurations. The results of these machines are combined to create complete machine learning models. In addition, cloud computing is consistent with parallel techniques such as data parallelism, model parallelism, and pipeline parallelism, which allow for simultaneous processing across different machines. This method is essential for managing large datasets and developing robust AI applications in the healthcare field as described in Table 5.4 and Table 5.5.

To successfully implement distributed computing, it is necessary to implement specific hardware and software configurations. Careful planning is essential to ensure smooth collaboration between machines and the optimal

Table 5.2 Summary of large-scale pretrained language models

Model	Number of parameters	Model architecture	Pretraining data	Training strategy	Training platform
DeBERTa$_{1.5B}$	1.5 billion	Encoder only	English data (78 GB)	—	PyTorch
T5	11 billion	Encoder–decoder (seq2seq)	C4 (750 GB)	Model/data parallelism	TensorFlow
GPT-3	175 billion	Decoder only	Cleaned CommonCrawl, WebText	Model parallelism	—
CPM	2.6 billion	Decoder only	Chinese corpus (100 GB)	—	PyTorch
PanGu-α	200 billion	Decoder only	Chinese data (1.1 TB, 250 billion tokens)	MindSpore autoparallel	MindSpore
ERNIE 3.0	10 billion	Encoder–decoder (unified)	Chinese data (4 TB), English data	Model/pipeline/tensor parallelism	PaddlePaddle
Turing-NLG	17 billion	Decoder only	English data	DeepSpeed/ZeRO	—
HyperCLOVA	204 billion	Decoder only	Korean data	—	—
CPM-2	11 billion	Encoder–decoder (seq2seq)	WuDao corpus (2.3 TB Chinese + 300 GB English)	—	PyTorch
CPM-2-MoE	198 billion	Encoder–decoder (seq2seq)	WuDao corpus (2.3 TB Chinese + 300 GB English)	Mixture of Experts (MoE)	PyTorch
Switch transformers	1751 billion	Encoder–decoder (seq2seq)	C4 (750 GB)	MoE	TensorFlow
Yuan 1.0	245 billion	Encoder–decoder (unified)	Chinese data (5 TB)	Model/pipeline/tensor parallelism	—
GLaM	1.2 trillion	Encoder only	English data (1.6 trillion tokens)	MoE/model parallelism	TensorFlow
Gopher	280 billion	Decoder only	English data (10.5 TB)	Model/data parallelism	Jax

(Wang et al., 2022)

Table 5.3 Large-scale multimodal PTMs

Model	Number of parameters	Pretraining paradigm	Pretraining data	Training parallelism	Training platform
DALL-E	12 billion	Denoising autoencoder	250 million English text–image pairs	Mixed-precision training	PyTorch
CogView	4 billion	Denoising autoencoder	30 million English text–image pairs	—	PyTorch
M6	100 billion	Causal language model	1.9 TB images + 292 GB Chinese text	Mixture of Experts (MoE)	—
ERNIE-ViLG	10 billion	Denoising autoencoder + Causal	145 million Chinese text–image pairs	Mixed-precision training	PaddlePaddle

(Wang et al., 2022)

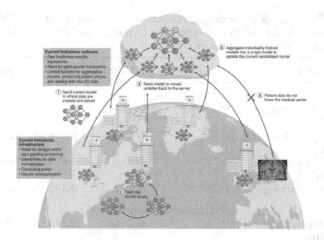

Figure 5.1 Cross-supervised learning in healthcare allows institutions to collaboratively train an ML model. Institutions notify a central server (step 1), train the model locally with their data (step 2), and return it to the server (step 3). The server aggregates the models into an updated version (step 4), which is repeated until training concludes while keeping patient data onsite (step 5). Successful implementation requires specialized frameworks and communication infrastructure (Zhang et al., 2022).

use of resources. Overall, cloud computing has not only accelerated machine learning processes but also dramatically improved the ability to analyze and discover information from complex medical data. See references: ("Gcore Named a Leader in 2024 GigaOm Radar for Edge Development Platforms", 2024) and (Zhang et al., 2022).

5.3.2 *Benefits of Parallel Processing in Model Training*

This parallel processing method offers many advantages for extending machine learning applications in the healthcare field. The use of distributed computing means that tasks are spread over several machines, allowing large assemblies to be managed, which a single machine cannot manage effectively. Data parallelism processes multiple datasets at the same time, whereas model parallelism distributes different elements of the model across different machines, which is essential for large-scale training when resources are limited to a single host. In addition, pipeline parallelism increases efficiency by allowing simultaneous manipulation of different steps in the model. This combination of distributed computing and parallel scanning increases the overall capacity of training materials by using interconnected computers or clusters. Each machine is responsible for forming a part of the data or model, which allows faster completion of tasks than a single scenario does. The collective results of all machines contribute to the final results, facilitating rapid model formation and improved scalability for healthcare applications. For proper implementation, appropriate equipment and software are required to

Table 5.4 Performance of the disease prediction models trained based on AUCCROC (area under the receiver operating characteristic curve) and AUCPR (area under the precision-recall curve)

Sample of Data	AUCROC	AUCPR	PPV	NPV
Diabetes				
Data with no separation (centralized)	0.824	0.526	0.620	0.809
Use only data with central analyzer	0.774	0.451	0.554	0.808
Federated learning using diagnosis*	0.775	0.465	0.614	0.809
Confederated learning	0.787	0.472	0.563	0.809
Psychological Disorders				
Data with no separation (centralized)	0.757	0.266	0.340	0.905
Use only data with central analyzer	0.647	0.163	0.230	0.903
Federated learning using diagnosis*	0.590	0.126	0.134	0.900
Confederated learning	0.718	0.239	0.356	0.909
Ischemic Heart Disease				
Data with no separation (centralized)	0.721	0.185	0.201	0.907
Use only data with central analyzer	0.679	0.160	0.197	0.907
Federated learning using diagnosis*	0.657	0.151	0.176	0.907
Confederated learning	0.698	0.169	0.199	0.909

PPV (positive predictive value); NPV (negative predictive value) using confederated learning on medical data distributed in 99 silos separated by individual, data type, and identity.
*As models obtained from federated learning for diagnosis performed better than models trained on medications or lab tests did, only the results of the models trained on diagnoses are shown (Liu et al., 2022).

Table 5.5 Analysis of conventional decentralized models with FL models concerning security aspects

Attributes	Conventional distributed models	Federated learning-driven models
Model data	Original data repository	Meta data and feature related information
Security cControl	Service provider	End users
Data controller	Service provider, end users	End users
Computational resources	Third-party, end users	Proprietary, end users
Network optimizer	Third-party	Proprietary
Fault tolerance	Centrally managed	Locally managed
Regulatory compliance	Less feasible	More feasible

(Srinivasu et al., 2024)

manage these procedures effectively. In summary, the integration of distributed computing and parallel processing frameworks has a significant effect on the efficiency and speed of model building on large amounts of medical data. Using these methods, healthcare organizations can overcome scalability challenges and achieve improved outcomes through the use of advanced machine learning models. See references: ("Gcore Named a Leader in 2024 GigaOm Radar for Edge Development Platforms", 2024) and (Srinivasu et al., 2024).

5.4 Transfer Learning and Fine-tuning Methods

5.4.1 Understanding Transfer Learning in Healthcare Applications

Transfer learning and "Fine-tuning" (Table 5.6) have revolutionized healthcare applications, particularly in the classification of medical images. By using information derived from pretrained models developed on large datasets such

Table 5.6 Comparative analysis of pretraining and fine-tuning in large language models (LLMs). The table delineates the principal distinctions between the pretraining and fine-tuning phases across several dimensions, including definitions, data prerequisites, objectives, methodologies, model adjustments, computational expenses, training durations, and their respective functions, accompanied by examples illustrating particular models and tasks. Pretraining entails comprehensive training on large quantities of unlabeled data to establish overall language proficiency, whereas fine-tuning modifies the pretrained models for specialized tasks utilizing smaller, labeled datasets, emphasizing enhancements in task-specific performance

Aspect	Pretraining	Fine-tuning
Definition	Training on a vast amount of unlabeled text data	Adapting a pretrained model to specific tasks
Data requirement	Extensive and diverse unlabeled text data	Smaller, task-specific labeled data
Objective	Build general linguistic knowledge	Specialize model for specific tasks
Process	Data collection, training on large dataset, predict next word/sequence	Collect task-specific data, adjust the final layer for the task, train on the new dataset, and produce output according to the tasks.
Model modification	Entire model trained	Last layers adapted for new task
Computational cost	High (large dataset, complex model)	Lower (smaller dataset, fine-tuning layers)
Training duration	Weeks to months	Days to weeks
Purpose	General language understanding	Task-specific performance improvement
Examples	GPT, LLaMA 3	Fine-tuning LLaMA 3 for summarization

(The Ultimate Guide to Fine-Tuning LLMs from Basics to Breakthroughs: An Exhaustive Review of Technologies, Research, Best Practices, Applied Research Challenges and Opportunities, 2024)

as ImageNet, this technique allows the adaptation of these models to new tasks even with limited labeled data. Therefore, knowledge transfer minimizes the need to rely on large datasets and high-performance computing resources, making it a cost-effective approach for medical imaging.

In the field of medical image classification, knowledge transfer has been successfully applied in areas such as the histological analysis of breast cancer and the detection of pulmonary nodules via computed tomography. The implementation of pretrained models in collaborative learning frameworks has yielded promising results in improving model performance while ensuring data privacy. Techniques such as convolutional neural networks (CNNs), combined with features such as the gray-level co-occurrence matrix (GLCM) and local binary patterns (LBP), have notably improved the accuracy and efficiency of medical image classification systems.

The main advantage of knowledge transfer is its ability to transfer learned information from one domain to another, which accelerates the training and deployment of models in clinical settings. The demand for precise and effective medical imaging solutions is increasing, and knowledge transfer is becoming an essential tool for healthcare professionals and researchers, enabling them to provide better diagnostic capabilities and improve patient care outcomes. The following references were used: (Li et al., 2021) and (Srinivasu et al., 2024).

5.4.2   Fine-tuning Pretrained Models for Specialized Tasks

Specialized fine-tuning of pretrained models is essential to optimize performance in resource-constrained healthcare applications. A major means is transfer learning, where models pretrained on datasets such as ImageNet are adapted to specific tasks. This method reduces the importance of classification and data formation, which reduces development and implementation costs. For example, adjusting only the last block of residual layers in a network can significantly improve efficiency while maintaining competitive performance.

Advanced techniques such as the weight-decomposed low-rank (DoRA) adaptation further enhance the fine-tuning of large language models. DoRA separates the magnitude and direction optimization processes, reproducing complete fine-tuning models while reducing the IT requirements. By reorganizing weight matrices into different elements for updates, DoRA improves model learning and flexibility while maintaining performance.

Half fine-tuning (HFT) combines the preservation of essential knowledge acquired during pretraining with the acquisition of task-specific skills. By blocking half of the model parameters at each stage of development, HFT preserves existing capabilities while allowing new ones to be integrated. This method ensures high performance in general tasks while reducing memory usage and computing costs.

In summary, the use of innovative fine-tuning techniques can significantly improve the scalability and efficiency of machine learning models in the healthcare sector. By combining transfer learning with advanced adaptive approaches such as DoRA and HFT, healthcare professionals can achieve impressive results with little data and computing resources. See references: ("The Ultimate Guide to Fine-tuning LLMs from Basics to Breakthroughs" (Table 5.7): "An Exhaustive Review of Technologies, Research, Best Practices, Applied Research Challenges, and Opportunities (Version 1.0)", 2024), and (Li et al., 2021).

5.5 Case Studies and Examples

5.5.1 Real-world Applications of Scaled Machine Learning Models in Healthcare

The use of machine learning models in real healthcare situations highlights the significant impact of using large databases and advanced training methods. A study of federal health learning revealed that models developed from data from multiple states performed better than those produced by individuals. The superior performance was particularly visible in environments with larger samples, highlighting the benefits of collaborative learning methods in health systems. In addition, comparison experiments on deep learning models revealed that MMDL deep models were more effective than Super Learner models, leading to an average improvement of 4–5% in the ICD-9 code prediction tasks. This discovery highlights the importance of using distributed data and effective model training methods to improve prediction capabilities and optimize health outcomes. See references: (Purushotham et al., 2018) and (Liu et al., 2022).

5.5.2 Successful Implementation Stories and Results

The use of large-scale machine learning models in healthcare has yielded promising results, notably with the RBP-TSTL framework for large-scale prediction of RNA-bound proteins (RBPs). Using a two-stage learning transfer method, RBP-TSTL was more effective than nine advanced techniques across different forms, demonstrating its effectiveness in predicting RBPs. The model's ability to leverage knowledge from pretraining datasets and generate relevant embeddings through supervised learning played a major role in its success. It was found to be resilient, offering superior prediction capabilities even when annotated data were limited.

RBP-TSTL was used specifically to predict potential RBPs in four target species: *Homo sapiens, Arabidopsis thaliana, Escherichia coli,* and Salmonella. By carefully selecting and calibrating to adjust confidence levels, the model identified tens of thousands of potential RBPs, highlighting different levels of certainty for each species. This rigorous methodology not only highlights the accuracy of the prediction model but also emphasizes its extensive use in genetic and protology studies.

In summary, the use of scalable machine learning models such as RBP-TSTL highlights their considerable potential to transform healthcare

Table 5.7 Thorough examination of obstacles in the initialization of a large language model (LLM). This table highlights essential factors, including the necessity of matching pretrained models with particular tasks, comprehending model design and compatibility, addressing resource limitations, and protecting data privacy. Furthermore, it addresses the issues associated with cost, maintenance, and the intricacies of model size, quantization, and bias recognition. Each problem is linked to detailed references to guarantee comprehensive comprehension and appropriate model implementation

Challenge	Description
Alignment with the target task	It is imperative that the pretrained model closely corresponds to your particular task or domain. This preliminary alignment establishes a robust basis for subsequent refinement endeavors, resulting in enhanced efficiency and outcomes.
Understanding the pretrained model	Prior to selecting a selection, it is essential to fully understand the architecture, functionalities, constraints, and the tasks for which the model was first trained. In the absence of this comprehension, fine-tuning endeavors may fail to produce the anticipated results.
Availability and compatibility	Thorough examination of a model's documentation, licensing, maintenance, and update frequency is essential to prevent potential complications and guarantee seamless integration into your application.
Model architecture	Not all models perform exceptionally in every task. Each model architecture possesses distinct advantages and disadvantages; therefore, choosing one that aligns with your own task is crucial for optimal results..
Resource constraints	Loading pretrained large language models is resource-intensive and necessitates increased computational power. These models require high-performance CPUs and GPUs, as well as substantial disk capacity. The Llama 3 8B model necessitates a minimum of 16GB of RAM for loading and executing inference.
Privacy	Privacy and confidentiality are essential considerations when choosing a large language model (LLM). Numerous enterprises opt against disclosing their data to external LLM providers. In these situations, deploying an LLM on local servers or utilizing pretrained LLMs from private cloud providers can be effective alternatives. These methods guarantee that data is retained within the company's facilities, thus safeguarding privacy and confidentiality.
Cost and maintenance	Hosting LLMs on local servers requires considerable effort and expense for both initial setup and continuous maintenance. Conversely, employing cloud suppliers mitigates resource maintenance difficulties but results in monthly billing expenses. These fees are generally determined by parameters such as model dimensions and the frequency of requests per minute.

(Continued)

Table 5.7 (*Continued*)

Challenge	Description
Model size and quantization	Utilizing a pretrained model with high memory usage can remain feasible by employing its quantized variant. Quantization allows for the loading of pretrained weights with decreased precision, often 4-bit or 8-bit floating point, significantly decreasing parameter volume while preserving substantial accuracy.
Pretraining datasets	Analyze the datasets employed for pretraining to assess the model's comprehension of language. These are significant since specific models exist for code generation, and we should avoid utilizing those models for finance text classification.
Bias awareness	Exercise caution with possible biases in pretrained models, particularly where unbiased predictions are essential. Bias awareness can be assessed by evaluating several models and backtracking the datasets utilized for pretraining..

(The Ultimate Guide to Fine-Tuning LLMs from Basics to Breakthroughs: An Exhaustive Review of Technologies, Research, Best Practices, Applied Research Challenges and Opportunities, 2024)

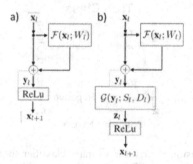

Figure 5.2 Residual block a) without and b) with deep representation scaling layers to improve information flow in the pretrained ResNet101 model (Byra, 2021).

applications. Using advanced methods such as transfer learning and effective training on large datasets, these models allow for in-depth knowledge of complex biological processes, opening the way for significant progress in health outcomes. See reference: (Peng & Wang, 2022).

5.6 Challenges and Future Directions

5.6.1 Addressing Scalability Challenges in Healthcare Machine Learning

Addressing scalability issues in medical machine learning is essential for integrating advanced models into real-world situations. An essential element is the importance of having large, well-structured, and diverse data to improve the effectiveness of the model. Despite the importance of model optimization, data quality is critical for obtaining reliable results. However, challenges arise due to limited data availability, patient privacy concerns, and various institutional data systems.

With the shift from machine learning systems to medical environments, emphasis has been placed on model implementation, highlighting the importance of data transmission for smooth workflow integration and early medical predictions. In addition, maintaining the model's resilience to changing physician and patient behaviors complicates scalability efforts. This underscores the importance of effective data management and accessibility to ensure the successful implementation of machine learning in health.

Regulation also plays an important role in the application of machine learning models in healthcare. Current rules are evolving to meet new requirements, such as data transformation and the inclusion of patients in training datasets. Complex models such as adversarial generative networks (GANs) and federated learning and transformation models add levels of complexity to regulatory assessments based on metrics evaluations described in Figure 5.3, Figure 5.4, Table 5.8, and Table 5.9, respectively. The lack of

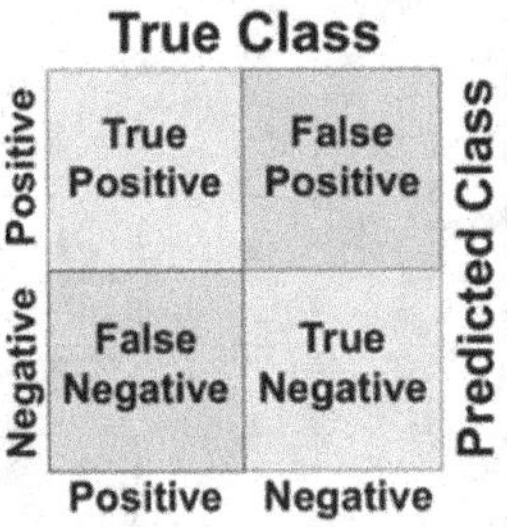

True Class

	Positive	Negative	
Positive	True Positive	False Positive	**Predicted Class**
Negative	False Negative	True Negative	

Figure 5.3 A 2×2 confusion matrix for a binary classifier summarizing true positives (TPs), false positives (FPs), false negatives (FNs), and true negatives (TNs) (Ellis et al., 2022).

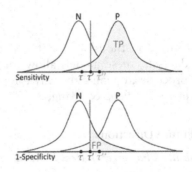

Figure 5.4 Two overlapping populations of negative (N) and positive (P) patients with a decision boundary at τ'. The top figure represents the portion of P correctly classified; the bottom represents the portion of N misclassified (Ellis et al., 2022).

Table 5.8 Defining accuracy, sensitivity (true positive rate), 1-specificity (false positive rate), and precision (positive predictive value) in terms of true positive (TP), false positive (FP), false negative (FN), and true negative (TN), given the true positives (P) and true negatives (N)

Metric	Formula	Description
Accuracy	$\dfrac{TP + TN}{P + N}$	The percentage of samples correctly identified as true positives and negatives.
True positive rate (sensitivity or recall)	$\dfrac{TP}{P}$	Of all samples in the positive class, what percentage are correctly identified.
False positive rate (1-specificity)	$\dfrac{FP}{N}$	Of all samples in the negative class, what percentage are incorrectly identified.
Positive predictive value (precision)	$\dfrac{TP}{TP + FP}$	Of all predictions for a given class, what percentage are correctly identified.

(Ellis et al., 2022)

Table 5.9 Machine learning models categorized into groups, including generalized linear models (GLMs), least absolute shrinkage and selection operators (LASSOs), principal component analysis (PCA), and t-distributed stochastic neighbor embedding (t-SNE). Certain approaches necessitate a limited number of hyperparameters, such as logistic regression (e.g., decision boundary threshold), whereas others demand a greater quantity, such as stepwise regression, which includes feature ranking, halting heuristics, complexity measurements, and so on

Regression	Distance-based	Tree-based	Neural networks	Others
GLM	Support vector machine	Classification/ Regression	Generative adversarial	Graphical model
Ridge/LASSO	Hierarchical clustering	Bagging and boosting	Convolutional	Belief network
Logistic	k-Nearest neighbors	Conditional decision	Autoencoder	Naïve Bayes
Stepwise	Manifold learner	Random forest	Transformer	PCA/t-SNE

(Ellis et al., 2022)

health-specific comparative data makes it even more difficult to assess the performance of machine learning systems in clinical applications. In summary, to address the scalability challenges in the field of medical machine learning, it is necessary to adopt a comprehensive approach that addresses barriers related to data collection, ensures efficient data transmission for model execution, maintains the resilience of the model to changing medical contexts, and manages regulatory changes. By focusing on these critical areas, health care institutions can effectively improve machine learning models to improve patient outcomes. See reference: (Zhang et al., 2022).

5.6.2 *Emerging Trends and Technologies for Scaling ML Models*

The landscape of machine learning in healthcare is constantly evolving with new trends and technologies aimed at extending models for real-world applications. A major phenomenon is networked learning, which allows multiple healthcare facilities to collaborate on models without sharing sensitive data, ensuring confidentiality. An example of this is the federal tumor segmentation initiative, which focuses on model aggregation and data standardization across different institutions.

In addition, supervised learning and foundation models are increasingly used in medical imaging tasks. These models, developed from many samples, offer a flexible approach that requires little supervision when adapting to new medical environments. The REMEDIS framework illustrates progress in generalizing data for medical imaging, facilitating more fluid implementation in different healthcare cases.

In addition, advances in transfer learning methods play a critical role in personalizing medicine, thus providing the opportunity to create personalized models at the hospital and cohort scales. By refining learning transfer techniques, the challenge of extending initial training data to other sites can be effectively addressed, thereby enhancing the adaptability of the model to local contexts. In summary, the adoption of innovative technologies such as federated learning, supervised learning, and transferred learning is essential to extend machine learning models into healthcare. Including these advanced methods can significantly improve patient management, simplify healthcare procedures, and lead to significant improvements in healthcare outcomes. See references: ("Robust and Efficient Medical Imaging with Self-supervision", 2024) and (Zhang et al., 2022).

5.7 Conclusion

Expanding the use of machine learning in healthcare can significantly benefit from collaborative frameworks that enable models to be trained on diverse datasets from various regions. This study demonstrates that models trained on multi-source data consistently outperform those relying solely on centralized data, particularly for key performance indicators such as AUC-ROC and AUCPR. This improvement likely results from the larger sample sizes made available through collaborative environments, suggesting that institutions with substantial patient data can maximize their contributions by joining a shared network. Therefore, scalability is crucial for effective medical machine learning applications, as collaborative training on large datasets can substantially enhance model performance. Broadening the deployment of machine learning models in healthcare is essential for improving patient outcomes. Training these models on various datasets, particularly within collaborative learning frameworks, leads to enhanced performance. Studies indicate that leveraging data from multiple sources within a collaborative network increases model efficacy over single-source data, as it allows models to learn from a broader patient population. Implementing distributed and parallel processing frameworks is key to effectively refining machine learning models. Additionally, cloud computing technologies facilitate efficient data handling and training processes for large-scale medical datasets, whereas transfer learning and fine-tuning techniques are vital for adapting models to specific healthcare tasks. In conclusion, machine learning models have the potential to significantly improve healthcare outcomes. By leveraging diverse datasets, distributed processing frameworks, and advanced modeling techniques, healthcare quality can be elevated, fostering ongoing innovation within the field.

References

Alzubaidi, L., Zhang, J., Humaidi, A. J., Al-Dujaili, A., Duan, Y., Al-Shamma, O., Santamaría, J., Fadhel, M. A., Al-Amidie, M., & Farhan, L. (2021). Review of deep learning: concepts, CNN architectures, challenges, applications, future directions. *Journal of Big Data*, 8(1). https://doi.org/10.1186/s40537-021-00444-8

Byra, M. (2021). Breast mass classification with transfer learning based on scaling of deep representations. *Biomedical Signal Processing and Control*, 69, 102828. https://doi.org/10.1016/j.bspc.2021.102828

Ellis, R. J., Sander, R. M., & Limon, A. (2022). Twelve key challenges in medical machine learning and solutions. *Intelligence-Based Medicine*, 100068. https://doi.org/10.1016/j.ibmed.2022.100068

Gcore named a Leader in 2024 GigaOm Radar for Edge Development Platforms. (2024). https://gcore.com/learning/large-scale-ai-model-training/

Li, F., Jin, Y., Liu, W., Rawat, B. P. S., Cai, P., & Yu, H. (2019). Fine-tuning bidirectional encoder representations from transformers (BERT)–based models on large-scale electronic health record notes: An empirical study. *JMIR Medical Informatics*, 7(3), e14830. https://doi.org/10.2196/14830

Li, J., Wang, P., Zhou, Y., Liang, H., & Luan, K. (2021). Different machine learning and deep learning methods for the classification of colorectal cancer lymph node metastasis images. *Frontiers in Bioengineering and Biotechnology*, 8. https://doi.org/10.3389/fbioe.2020.620257

Liu, D., Fox, K., Weber, G., & Miller, T. (2022). Confederated learning in healthcare: training machine learning models using disconnected data separated by individual, data type and identity for Large-Scale Health System Intelligence. *Journal of Biomedical Informatics*, 104151. https://doi.org/10.1016/j.jbi.2022.104151

Peng, X., Wang, X., Guo, Y., Ge, Z., Li, F., Gao, X., & Song, J. (2022). RBP-TSTL is a two-stage transfer learning framework for genome-scale prediction of RNA-binding proteins. *Briefings in Bioinformatics*, 23(4). https://doi.org/10.1093/bib/bbac215

Purushotham, S., Meng, C., Che, Z., & Liu, Y. (2018). Benchmarking deep learning models on large healthcare datasets. *Journal of Biomedical Informatics*, 83, 112–134. https://doi.org/10.1016/j.jbi.2018.04.007

Robust and efficient medical imaging with self-supervision. (2024). http://research.google/blog/robust-and-efficient-medical-imaging-with-self-supervision/

Sarker, I. H. (2021). Machine learning: Algorithms, real-world applications and research directions. *SN Computer Science*, 2(3), 1–21. https://doi.org/10.1007/s42979-021-00592-x

Srinivasu, N. P., Jaya Lakshmi, G., Canavoy Narahari, S., Shafi, J., Choi, J., & Fazal Ijaz, M. (2024). Enhancing medical image classification via federated learning and pretrained model. *Egyptian Informatics Journal*, 27, 100530. https://doi.org/10.1016/j.eij.2024.100530

The Ultimate Guide to Fine-Tuning LLMs from Basics to Breakthroughs: An Exhaustive Review of Technologies, Research, Best Practices, Applied Research Challenges and Opportunities (Version 1.0). (2024). Arxiv.org. https://arxiv.org/html/2408.13296v1

Vora, L. K., Gholap, A. D., Jetha, K., Thakur, R. R. S., Solanki, H. K., & Chavda, V. P. (2023). Artificial intelligence in pharmaceutical technology and drug delivery design. *Pharmaceutics*, 15(7), 1916–1916. https://doi.org/10.3390/pharmaceutics15071916

Wang, H., Li, J., Wu, H., Hovy, E., & Sun, Y. (2022). Pre-trained language models and their applications. *Engineering*. https://doi.org/10.1016/j.eng.2022.04.024

Zhang, A., Xing, L., Zou, J., & Wu, J. C. (2022). Shifting machine learning for healthcare from development to deployment and from models to data. *Nature Biomedical Engineering*. https://doi.org/10.1038/s41551-022-00898-y

6 Deployment and Continuous Integration of AI in Healthcare

Houneida Sakly, Ramzi Guetari, and Naoufel Kraiem

6.1 Introduction

6.1.1 Overview of AI Deployment in Healthcare

The rapid growth of artificial intelligence (AI) in healthcare offers many benefits, such as personalized experiences for patients, improved outcomes, and enhanced skills for practitioners. However, integrating AI tools into the healthcare field also presents many challenges, such as meeting production deadlines, developing trust, addressing confidentiality issues, reducing algorithmic biases, and managing data constraints. The simple implementation of AI does not solve the deep-seated problems associated with business models and work processes; it requires a fundamental reassessment of healthcare operations. Turning AI's vision into an asset is critical to improving healthcare delivery and exploring new opportunities.

The successful integration of artificial intelligence requires more than financial investments; it requires special attention to continuing education and the creation of a supportive environment. Effective legislation is crucial to building trust and ensuring ethical practices in AI by creating frameworks that address transparency, model accuracy, data reliability, accountability issues, and ethical considerations. An increased understanding of artificial intelligence within educational institutions is essential to prepare future healthcare professionals for an AI-enabled environment. By proactively addressing these challenges and taking a prudent approach, the healthcare sector can fully harness the transformative potential of artificial intelligence. This will transform the delivery of care and improve patient management while managing associated risks. The future of healthcare, in conjunction with artificial intelligence, is based on intentional engagement and innovative strategies that offer many benefits to organizations, professionals, and patients. See references: ("AI Deployment Journey in Healthcare: Governance, Design, and Adoption", 2024; Beavins, 2024; Esmaeilzadeh, 2024; Esmaeilzadeh, 2024).

6.1.2 Importance of CI/CD Pipelines

Continuous integration/continuous deployment (CI/CD) practices play a critical role in advancing artificial intelligence in the healthcare sector.

DOI: 10.1201/9781003480594-6

By automating integration, testing and deployment, CI/CD pipelines enable continuous improvements in artificial intelligence models. With this synergy between CI/CD and AI, healthcare institutions can quickly develop, validate, and implement AI models while meeting legal requirements. Automated pipelines enable rapid validation of model improvements and effective monitoring of model performance in real-time. By integrating CI/CD into the development process, health organizations can achieve faster turnaround times, continuous feedback mechanisms, improved software quality, and reduced development costs. The seamless integration of CI/CD ensures that artificial intelligence systems retain their robustness, reliability, and ability to adapt to changing conditions in healthcare environments(Yarlagadda et al., 2017).

6.2 Continuous Integration and Deployment (CI/CD) in Healthcare

6.2.1 *Explanation of CI/CD Pipelines*

Continuous integration and deployment (CI/CD) methods play a key role in the evolution of artificial intelligence solutions in the healthcare sector. This practice facilitates the smooth integration of artificial intelligence models into clinical environments through effective implementation procedures. CI/CD pipelines automate the integration, testing, and implementation of artificial intelligence models, enabling continuous improvement, comprehensive testing, and simplified deployment. By adopting CI/CD principles, healthcare organizations can improve their development processes, allowing faster iteration, quicker validation, and regular standard compliance.

CI/CD pipelines can significantly accelerate implementation by automating testing procedures, ensuring the robustness and reliability of artificial intelligence models before they are implemented. They are designed to handle large amounts of data and complex calculations, making them essential for expanding AI operations in the healthcare field. In addition, CI/CD methods promote collaboration among data researchers, machine learning engineers and developers (Zhang et al., 2022). This collaborative approach enables the creation of scalable and sustainable artificial intelligence solutions for medical applications as described in Table 6.1 and Table 6.2.

6.2.2 *Benefits of Using CI/CD in Healthcare AI Deployment*

Continuous integration and deployment (CI/CD) are essential methods in developing artificial intelligence, particularly in the healthcare sector. They facilitate the smooth integration of AI models into medical environments through simplified implementation procedures. The CI/CD pipeline automates the integration, testing and deployment of artificial intelligence models, enabling continuous improvement and in-depth validation. This approach allows healthcare institutions to streamline the AI solution development process, allowing faster iteration and regular standard compliance.

Table 6.1 Summary of key information from each research topic manuscript

Name	Institution	Country	Model use case	Manuscript objective	AI translation phase	Key takeaways
An Integration Engineering Framework for Machine Learning in Healthcare	The Hospital for Sick Children	Canada	Arrhythmia detection model integrated as best practice.	Presents a systems engineering framework to guide model development and integration, mitigating risks like inefficiency, patient harm, and system failure.	Develop ment; Technical Integration; Lifecycle Management	• Framework covers technical, human, and environmental system domains. • Conducted narrative review on ML integration challenges and SDLC gaps. • Four phases: Inception, Preparation, Development, Integration.
Clinical Deployment Environments: Five Pillars of Translational Machine Learning for Health	University College London Hospital	UK	Real-time NOAF prediction using electrolytes, medications, and patient comorbidities.	Describes functional requirements for Clinical Deployment Environments (CDE), ensuring algorithms receive similar stewardship to medicines and medical devices.	Develop ment; Technical Integration; Lifecycle Management	Five pillars: real-world development, ML-Ops, responsible AI, implementation science, continuous evaluation. Explains similarities between ML translation and drug development. Details on the EMAP and FlowEHR platforms for iterative model testing and deployment.

(Continued)

Table 6.1 Summary of key information from each research topic manuscript (*Continued*)

Name	Institution	Country	Model use case	Manuscript objective	AI translation phase	Key takeaways
The Silent Trial: A Bridge Between Bench-to-Bedside AI Applications	The Hospital for Sick Children	Canada	Predicts obstruction in hydronephrotic kidneys using ultrasound.	Highlights lessons from validating AI through a silent trial, addressing dataset drift, bias, feasibility, and stakeholder attitudes.	Technical Integration; Clinical Integration	• Two-step silent trial for prospective generalization and retraining. • Updated model to mitigate dataset shift. Assessed patient and family perceptions of AI postvisit.
Operationalizing a Real-Time Fall Risk Model in the Emergency Department	University of Wisconsin Health	USA	Predicts fall risk among older adults based on EHR data.	Describes the challenges of transitioning an EHR-based model from research to real-time operation.	Technical Integration; Clinical Integration	Model development in three stages over 15 months. Discussed IT constraints, interpretability, and workflow integration. Modified model placement and thresholds for better adoption.
Deploying an Early Warning System in Clinical Practice	St. Michael's Hospital	Canada	CHARTwatch predicts inpatient deterioration for ICU transfers or death.	Details infrastructure setup and deployment insights, comparing practices to GMLP guidelines.	Technical Integration; Clinical Integration	Minimized alert fatigue with snooze and alert silencing features. Adapted model post-silent trial to high sensitivity troponin. Established downtime protocols and end-user engagement practices.

Title	Institution	Country	Application	Description	Category	Key Points
Reliability and Fairness Audits for Predictive Models in Advance Care Planning	Stanford Health Care	USA	Assessed models for 12-month mortality prediction to support ACP.	Designs and reported a reliability and fairness audit, identifying performance variations across demographic subgroups.	Lifecycle Management	• Audited two models for calibration and fairness. Surveyed decision-makers on audit results and adoption impact. • Quantified audit effort (115 hours) and resource needs.
Monitoring and Updating AI-Enabled Tools in Clinical Settings	Vanderbilt University Medical Center	USA	Evaluated models predicting readmission (LACE+) and suicide risk (VSAIL).	Highlights the importance of maintaining predictive models and discusses performance drift in operational environments.	Lifecycle Management	• Presented performance drift patterns using O ratios. • Explored model maintenance policies, monitoring perspectives, and update strategies. Discussed ownership and control of model maintenance.
Governance for Safe AI Deployment in a Large Health System	University of Wisconsin Health	USA	AI models deployed for various tasks (e.g., sepsis detection, opioid abuse screening).	Describes the development of governance structures to oversee AI adoption, ensuring safety and equity.	Full Lifecycle	• Established Clinical AI and Predictive Analytics Committee. • Developed five guiding principles for governance. Detailed ongoing monitoring, model retirement, and incorporation of equity concerns.

(Continued)

Table 6.1 Summary of key information from each research topic manuscript (*Continued*)

Name	Institution	Country	Model use case	Manuscript objective	AI translation phase	Key takeaways
A Quality Management System for AI/ML-Based Clinical Decision Support	University Medical Center Utrecht	Netherlands	"Sleep Well Baby" model monitors sleep-wake patterns in preterm neonates.	Illustrates quality management processes for AI/ML tools, guided by ISO standards and regulations.	Full Lifecycle	• Created a 7-phase innovation funnel for AI development. • Applied IEC 62304 and ISO 14971 standards. Addressed lifecycle management questions (e.g., model ownership, user training, change management).

Table 6.2 Commonly used clinical datasets

Dataset	Data types	Size of the dataset	Institutions	Applications
Multimodal braintumor image—segmentation benchmark dataset (BRATS)	Multiparametric MRI: T1, T1Gd, T2 and T2-FLAIR	~2,000 patients; ~8,000 scans	Multi-institution (13)	GANs: image-to-image translation Federated learning
Alzheimer's disease neuroimaging initiative dataset (ADNI)	MRI, PET Genetics, cognitive tests and biomarkers	~2,000 patients	Multi-institution (63)	GANs: data augmentation, anonymization, image-to-image translation Federated learning
Autism brain imaging data exchange	Functional MRI	~1,114 patients	Multi-institution (19)	Federated learning
NIH prostate, lung, colorectal, and ovarian cancer dataset (NIH PLCO)	X-ray images (chest) Digital histopathology (prostate, lung, colorectal, ovarian, breast, and bladder) Questionnaires and laboratory data	~155,000 patients	NCI	GANs
Medical segmentation decathlon	MRI images (brain, heart and prostate) CT images (lung, liver, spleen, pancreas, colon, hepatic vessels and prostate)	~2,633 images	Multi-institution	Federated learning
NIH DeepLesion	CT images	~4,400 patients; ~32,000 lesions	NIH	Federated learning
Cancer imaging archive	MRI, CT, PET and digital histopathology Multiorgan	~1,000–3,000 patients	Multi-institution	GANs
Medical information mart for intensive care (MIMIC)	Electronic medical records	~60,000 patients	Beth Israel Deaconess Medical Center	Clinical text and events modeling Federated learning
IBM MarketScan research databases for life-science researchers	Electronic medical records and claims	~43.6 million	Multi-institution	Federated learning
EchoNet-Dynamic	Echocardiogram videos	~10,030 videos	Stanford Health Care	Video-based segmentation and classification; largest publicly available medical video dataset

The automation of test procedures ensures that AI models are robust and reliable before they are implemented (De Silva et al., 2022).

They have the ability to handle large amount of data and perform complex calculations typical of AI projects, which promote scalability in medical AI applications. In addition, CI/CD methods promote collaboration among data researchers, machine learning engineers and developers. Adding continuous integration and delivery to the workflow fosters collaboration, leading to the creation of scalable and sustainable artificial intelligence solutions for medical environments. Overall, CI/CD pipelines are critical to the effective implementation of AI in healthcare, enabling companies to advance model deployment while maintaining reliability and compliance standards. By integrating these methods into the software development process (SDLC) of healthcare solutions, teams can ensure successful and smooth integration of artificial intelligence models into key workflows (Steidl et al., 2023; Yarlagadda et al., 2017).

6.3   Best Practices for Monitoring Deployed Models

6.3.1   *Importance of Monitoring Models in Healthcare Settings*

In the healthcare sector, monitoring AI models is essential to ensure their safety, reliability, and effectiveness. Continuous monitoring is crucial for performance evaluation and the detection of potential problems that may arise after implementation. Collaboration among developers, healthcare professionals, and regulators is vital for addressing ethical issues and maintaining a continuous assessment of AI performance.

By implementing monitoring strategies that involve regular reassessments and continuous performance monitoring, healthcare institutions can proactively identify data fluctuations that may impact the model's effectiveness over time. Continuous monitoring solutions provide real-time feedback on model performance, facilitating rapid responses to deviations. This proactive approach is essential to ensure patient safety and maintain the effectiveness of artificial intelligence applications in clinical practice.

Protocols for the ongoing monitoring of artificial intelligence are essential for quickly detecting negative outcomes and ensuring the continued effectiveness of AI tools in real-world situations. Ultimately, the ongoing monitoring of AI models is a critical element for responsible AI implementation in healthcare environments. By adopting robust monitoring methods, healthcare organizations can maintain safety standards, optimize patient care delivery, and improve the overall effectiveness of AI technologies. See references: ("CI/CD for AI In Healthcare", 2024; Brady et al., 2024).

6.3.2   *Strategies for Effective Model Monitoring*

In the healthcare field, monitoring models are essential to ensure reliability and safety. Dr. Peter J. Embi of Vanderbilt University Medical Center highlighted the importance of testing models generated by artificial intelligence in different healthcare environments to reduce adverse consequences. An essential strategy for effective monitoring is to conduct regular performance assessments to evaluate the accuracy, calibration, and adaptability of models across different demographic groups. It is also essential to establish clear guidelines for model maintenance to address challenges such as data variations and performance declines over time. It is crucial to regularly evaluate the performance of the model in real clinical situations, use systematic methods to track results, detect anomalies, and implement timely updates or interventions.

Transparency and accountability in follow-up methods are essential to building trust between healthcare providers and patients. Regular reliability and fairness checks ensure the ethical and fair use of artificial intelligence tools. A comprehensive approach to model monitoring should include performance assessments, field trials, transparency initiatives, and ongoing management frameworks. By adopting these strategies, healthcare organizations can improve the effectiveness and safety of AI-based solutions, leading to improved patient outcomes (Sendak et al., 2023).

6.4   Managing Deployed Models for Performance, Reliability, and Compliance

6.4.1   Ensuring the Performance of AI Models in Healthcare

Ensuring the operational effectiveness of AI models in healthcare is essential to ensure safe and effective patient management. Clear roles and procedures need to be established in medical institutions to reduce the risk of errors that could harm patients. Given the importance of AI applications in healthcare, maintaining performance, reliability, and regulatory compliance is essential.

It is crucial to continuously monitor the AI models in place to improve operational efficiency. By implementing effective follow-up strategies, healthcare providers can proactively identify and address any changes in expected behaviors. This method preserves the accuracy of artificial intelligence results and enhances patient safety by detecting abnormalities that could lead to adverse outcomes.

In addition, the management of artificial intelligence models involves regularly updating these applications in response to new data and regulatory changes. This iterative process improves model performance while ensuring adherence to industry standards and best practices. By working with regulatory authorities and conducting in-depth legal assessments, healthcare institutions can implement up-to-date artificial intelligence solutions that adhere to current medical protocols.

In summary, maintaining the operational effectiveness of AI models in healthcare requires a proactive strategy focused on monitoring, updating, and managing compliance. By adopting these methods when they are implemented, healthcare providers can improve the effectiveness of AI applications

Table 6.3 Common QMS and medical device terminology

Installation qualification	Testing or evaluation activities that demonstrate the software is installed correctly in its intended environment.
Intended purpose (intended use)	The objective intent and general purpose of a product.
Operational qualification	Testing or evaluation activities that demonstrate the software functions as intended.
Performance qualification	Testing or evaluation activities that demonstrate the software satisfies user and business requirements.
Records	Documents or other artifacts that demonstrate that a process was completed.
Software Development Life Cycle (SDLC)	A framework of processes, activities, and tasks phases to design, develop, and maintain software.
Monitoring and surveillance	Tracking and analyzing the performance of and changes to products after deployment to identify quality or safety issues that may necessitate corrective or preventive action.
Version control	Activity related to software configuration management intended to track and manage changes to software. Version control is used during all stages of the software development life cycle to prevent mix-ups.

while ensuring patient safety and compliance with legal obligations. The Common QMS and Medical Device Terminology table provides a description of essential terms in Quality Management Systems (QMS) and medical device regulations, such as "ISO 13485" (a standard for medical device quality management), "CAPA" (Corrective and Preventive Action), and "CE Marking" (EU compliance certification) as shown in Table 6.3. This resource helps professionals ensure a unified understanding of regulatory language, supporting consistent quality and safety in medical device production and compliance. See references: (Sailesh Conjeti, 2023; Shakya, 2023; Hofmann et al., 2024).

6.4.2 *Maintaining Reliability and Compliance Standards*

Ensuring reliability and compliance with AI healthcare regulations is critical to safeguarding patient well-being and data security. Clearly defined roles and clear integration procedures are essential to ensure that artificial intelligence systems function properly. Accounting for AI-influenced health outcomes highlights the importance of strong surveillance and regulatory compliance. The potential risks associated with AI applications, such as privacy concerns and social consequences, underscore the importance of ethical oversight and responsible management.

Integrating established medical protocols into the use of AI is essential to meet legal requirements and ensure patient safety. The evaluation of new protocols should involve a multidisciplinary team of specialists to ensure the reliability and effectiveness of AI models. An overall approach that takes into account technical, medical, and regulatory aspects is essential to maintain high standards of performance and reliability in the healthcare field.

The success of artificial intelligence applications requires taking into account social, ethical, and legal aspects to promote patient-centered management and safe use. It is essential to implement dedicated AI management methods that focus on transparency, safety, risk assessment, and patient confidence. By meeting management standards and implementing robust security measures, healthcare institutions can reduce the risks associated with the use of AI while fostering innovation and building public confidence. See reference: (Hofmann et al., 2024).

6.5 Integration of AI into the Software Development Life Cycle (SDLC)

6.5.1 Overview of the SDLC Process

The integration of artificial intelligence (AI) into the software development process (SDLC) has led to a transformation in software design, development, and maintenance. Artificial intelligence-based tools increase productivity and optimize outcomes at every step of the continuous development process (SDLC), from needs analysis to strategy design, by automating code, testing, and debugging as seen in Figure 6.1.

In the healthcare solutions field, organizations can leverage artificial intelligence to benefit from many advantages. Artificial intelligence can analyze large datasets, facilitating the precise definition of projects and risk assessment during planning. It also automates the creation and testing of code, which improves software quality and reduces errors throughout development. In

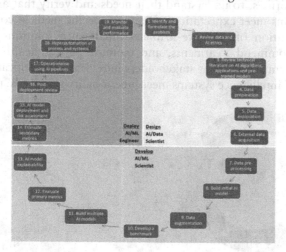

Figure 6.1 The CDAC AI life cycle: Three phases of (1) design, (2) develop, and (3) deploy, and 19 stages.

addition, AI simplifies implementation procedures and provides predictive maintenance analytics for ongoing monitoring and maintenance.

The evolution of AI in software development is challenging industry standards, with an increasing focus on AI-based methods. Developers have the opportunity to design more efficient software by using artificial intelligence skills through all stages of the SDLC. By adopting artificial intelligence from design to implementation, we are seeing a shift toward fully autonomous development environments. The integration of Artificial Intelligence (AI) into the software development lifecycle (SDLC) is revolutionizing how projects are delivered, particularly in complex Cyber–Physical Systems (CPSs). The AIDOaRT project, a European collaborative initiative, combines AI with Model Driven Engineering principles to improve system modeling, coding, testing, monitoring, and continuous development. AIDOaRT focuses on enhancing CPS engineering by offering AI-augmented solutions that analyze data in real-time and at design stages, ultimately leading to more reliable systems. This approach is expected to simplify procedures, enhance software quality, and increase user satisfaction, with a notable impact on sectors such as healthcare (Bruneliere et al., 2022).

6.5.2 Incorporating AI into the SDLC for Healthcare Solutions

The integration of artificial intelligence (AI) into the software development lifecycle (SDLC) for healthcare solutions follows a methodical approach to ensure reliability, efficiency, and compliance with regulations, as described in Figure 6.2. The process can be divided into three stages: machine learning (ML), software development (Dev), and operations (Ops). It is crucial to involve key stakeholders, such as healthcare professionals, patients, and regular authorities, to understand their needs and verify that artificial intelligence systems meet expectations. Defining specific medical concepts facilitates the creation of accurate artificial intelligence solutions to diagnose diseases, recommend treatments, and monitor patient health. Translating the requirements of relevant stakeholders into clear IT specifications ensures that artificial intelligence systems meet functionality standards, performance,

Figure 6.2 MLOps in healthcare for AI products.

safety, and regulatory requirements tailored to the specific needs of the healthcare industry. See reference: (Sailesh Conjeti, 2023).

6.6 Collaboration between AI Engineers and Developers

6.6.1 Collaboration between Teams

Effective collaboration is essential for the smooth implementation of artificial intelligence in healthcare settings. The implementation of artificial intelligence in healthcare requires collaboration between developers, healthcare professionals, regulatory authorities, and other stakeholders to address ethical issues and monitor AI performance, as described in Table 6.4. This collaboration helps identify early hazards, biases, and integration challenges before implementing the technology in medical environments, ensuring patient wellbeing and reducing risk. Interdisciplinary teams also play a critical role in the management and administration of AI, assigning roles, and ensuring the responsible use of AI models. Through interdisciplinary collaboration, teams can design long-term and sustainable solutions that meet rigorous medical standards while meeting ethical standards. See reference: (Brady et al., 2024).

6.6.2 Creating Scalable and Maintainable Solutions through Teamwork

To design effective and sustainable artificial intelligence solutions for healthcare, collaboration between AI engineers and developers is essential. This collaboration between experts from these two groups has led to the development of robust artificial intelligence systems that meet the complex requirements of healthcare environments. AI engineers gain expertise in artificial intelligence, data processing, and model development, whereas developers contribute their skills in software architecture, programming, and systems integration. By combining these strengths, teams can design AI solutions that are accurate, efficient, and reliable, and that meet industry standards.

Collaborative efforts optimize AI models to improve performance, scalability, and sustainability. Teams can address critical issues such as data security, privacy, and ethical considerations thoroughly. This ensures that artificial intelligence systems meet both the technical requirements and healthcare standards. Furthermore, encouraging a culture of collaboration fosters innovation by promoting knowledge sharing, continuous learning, and cross-functional communication. This enables companies to create dynamic teams capable of adapting to evolving technological and healthcare needs. Adaptability is key to designing resilient AI solutions that keep pace with developments in the healthcare delivery field. In short, AI engineers and developers must work together to design innovative and sustainable healthcare solutions. By harnessing the effective collaboration between the two teams, organizations can design cutting-edge AI systems that meet the rigorous standards required in healthcare environments. See references: (Overgaard et al., 2023; Jha, 2024; Sendak et al., 2023).

Table 6.4 An overview of the interviewees

Industry	Position	Organization	Background	Work experience	Country
Health AI	Software Developer	Research institution	Medical informatics (M.Sc.)	3–5 years	Germany
Regulatory	Managing of Partner, Professor Law	Law firm and research institution	Attorney and professor, medical law (PhD in law)	>20 years	Germany
Medical technology	ML Researcher	Startup	Computer science (PhD in engineering)	5–10 years	Germany
Medicine	Chief Physician	Hospital	Radiology (M.D. and reader)	10–15 years	Germany
Medical technology	Data Scientist	Startup	Chemistry (PhD in theoretical physics)	10–15 years	Germany
Health AI	AI Consultant	Enterprise	Service management and engineering (M.Sc.)	3–5 years	Germany
Medicine	Senior Physician, AI Researcher	Hospital	Radiology (M.D.)	10–15 years	Germany
Medicine	AI Researcher, Chief Strategic Officer	Hospital research institution and startup	Medicine (M.D, PhD in medical neuroscience, MA in medical ethics)	10–15 years	Germany
Health insurance	Digital Care Manager	Statutory health insurer	Economics (PhD in public economics)	5–10 years	Germany
Health AI	Director Medical Data Science	Enterprise	Bioinformatic s (PhD in data mining and ML)	5–10 years	Germany
Systems	Professor of Digital Management	Research institution	Digital management (PhD in information systems)	15–20 years	Germany

6.7 Case Studies and Examples of Healthcare AI Deployment

6.7.1 Real-world Examples of Successful AI Deployment in Healthcare

A concrete example of the application of artificial intelligence in the field of healthcare highlights its many benefits and applications. Canada has developed an engineering integration framework for machine learning, focusing on systems engineering to reduce costs and avoid harm to patients. This framework is used for tasks such as arrhythmia detection and hydronephrosis detection in children. At University College London, a critical setting environment (CDE) allows the use of translational machine learning to assess the real-time risk of new atrial arrhythmias via patient data. This highlights how artificial intelligence can improve clinical decision-making processes. Wisconsin Health University has implemented a real-time scoring model to predict the risk of dropout in older adults. Using an automated selection algorithm with machine learning and electronic health records, this initiative addresses the challenges of creating and verifying models, highlighting the importance of artificial intelligence in improving patient outcomes through proactive approaches to fall prevention. They highlight the critical importance of adopting AI technologies in healthcare settings. Through the use of strong AI and framework solutions, healthcare facilities can make progress in disease detection, treatment planning, and overall operational effectiveness, reducing patient outcomes and simplifying medical processes. See references: ("GE Healthcare Accelerates AI Model Development and Deployment with Launch of Edison Integration to American College of Radiology AI-LAB™", 2024; Sendak et al., 2023).

6.7.2 Lessons Learned from Case Studies to Inform Future Projects

It is crucial to highlight the importance of testing AI models in real healthcare situations before they are fully implemented. This approach allows for the identification of effective solutions and the assessment of model adaptability in different healthcare settings. In addition, it is essential to assess the practical utility of the AI models deployed. Healthcare leaders should monitor the effective integration of these models into existing processes and establish protocols for ongoing performance evaluation. Ongoing monitoring ensures that the AI system remains valuable and achieves its intended objectives. Working with industry leaders, healthcare providers, and regulators is critical to ensuring effective AI integration. By sharing good practices, setting standards, and providing tools for measuring outcomes, stakeholders can work together to make secure and equitable AI solutions accessible across the healthcare sector. Working with different stakeholders, such as public bodies, hospitals, end users, and manufacturers, can provide information that helps overcome challenges and improve implementation procedures. In summary, these case studies highlight the importance of rigorous testing, continuous monitoring, and collaboration among relevant stakeholders in the application of artificial intelligence in healthcare. By using lessons learned from past experiences, organizations can facilitate the integration of artificial technology into healthcare settings while ensuring safety, reliability, and improved patient outcomes. See references: (Gupta et al., 2022; Shah & Miller, 2022).

6.8 Conclusion

The deployment and integration of AI solutions in healthcare represent a transformative step toward enhancing the quality, efficiency, and reliability of patient care. By implementing Continuous Integration and Continuous Deployment (CI/CD) pipelines, healthcare organizations can ensure that AI models are updated seamlessly, reducing downtime and accelerating model iteration. This approach fosters a dynamic environment where models are continuously monitored, maintained, and fine-tuned to address issues like model drift, bias, and compliance requirements, thereby supporting optimal performance. Integrating AI into the Software Development Life Cycle (SDLC) and fostering collaboration between AI engineers, data scientists, and software developers are essential for creating scalable and sustainable AI solutions that meet the complex demands of healthcare settings. Such interdisciplinary efforts enable the development of robust systems that adapt to the unique regulatory and operational challenges of healthcare, promoting the responsible use of AI and ensuring patient safety. As AI continues to advance, the healthcare sector must adopt best practices for managing and maintaining deployed models, reinforcing a commitment to ethical standards, transparency, and continuous improvement. This chapter underscores the importance of aligning technological innovation with healthcare needs, offering a framework for deploying AI solutions that are not only effective but also reliable and sustainable in the long term.

References

AI Deployment Journey in Healthcare: Governance, Design, and Adoption. (2024). https://www.tilburguniversity.edu/about/digital-sciences-society/projects/ai-deploymentjourney-healthcare

Brady, A. P., Allen, B., Chong, J., Kotter, E., Kottler, N., Mongan, J., OakdenRayner, L., Pinto, D., Tang, A., Wald, C., & Slavotinek, J. (2024). Development, Purchasing, Implementing and Monitoring AI Tools in Radiology: Practical Considerations. A multi-society statement from the ACR, CAR, ESR, RANZCR and RSNA. *Radiology*, 6(1). https://doi.org/10.1148/ryai.230513

Bruneliere, H., Muttillo, V., Eramo, R., Berardinelli, L., Gómez, A., Bagnato, A., Sadovykh, A., & Cicchetti, A. (2022). AIDOaRt: AI-augmented automation for DevOps, a model-based framework for continuous development in cyber–physical systems. *Microprocessors and Microsystems*, 94, 104672. https://doi.org/10.1016/j.micpro.2022.104672

De Silva, D., & Alahakoon, D. (2022). An artificial intelligence life cycle: From conception to production. *Patterns*, 3(6), 100489. https://doi.org/10.1016/j.patter.2022.100489

Beavins, E. (2024). National Nurses United pushes back against deployment of 'unproven' AI in healthcare. https://www.fiercehealthcare.com/ai-and -machinelearning/national-nurses-united-pushes-back-against-deployment-ai -healthcare

Esmaeilzadeh, P. (2024). Challenges and strategies for wide-scale artificial intelligence (AI) deployment in healthcare practices: A perspective for healthcare organizations. *Artificial Intelligence in Medicine (Print)*, 151, 102861–102861. https://doi.org/10 .1016/j.artmed.2024.102861

GE Healthcare Accelerates AI Model Development and Deployment with Launch of Edison Integration to American College of Radiology AI-LAB™. (2024). https://www.gehealthcare.com/about/newsroom/press-releases/ge-healthcare -acceleratesai-model-development-and-deployment-launch-edison?npclid =botnpclid

Gupta, V., Erdal, B. S., Ramirez, C., Floca, R., Jackson, L., Genereaux, B., Bryson, S., Bridge, C. P., Kleesiek, J., Nensa, F., Braren, R., Younis, K., Penzkofer, T., Bucher, A. M., Qin, M. M., Bae, G., Lee, H., Jorge, C. M., Ourselin, S., & Kerfoot, E. (2022). Current state of community-driven radiological AI deployment in medical imaging. *ArXiv.org*. https://arxiv.org/abs/2212.14177

Hofmann, P., Lämmermann, L., & Urbach, N. (2024). Managing artificial intelligence applications in healthcare: Promoting information processing among stakeholders. *International Journal of Information Management*, 75, 102728. https://doi.org/10 .1016/j.ijinfomgt.2023.102728

Jha, R. (2024). Future of software development with generative AI & machine learning. https://www.linkedin.com/pulse/future-software-development-generative -aimachine-learning-rajoo-jha-ysyjc

Microsoft Source. (2024). A new consortium of healthcare leaders announced the formation of the Trustworthy & Responsible AI Network (TRAIN), making safe and fair AI accessible to every healthcare organization—Stories. https://news .microsoft.com/2024/03/11/newconsortium-of-healthcare-leaders-announces -formation-of-trustworthy-responsible-ainetwork-train-making-safe-and-fair-ai -accessible-to-every-healthcare-organization/

Overgaard, S. M., Graham, M. G., Brereton, T., Pencina, M. J., Halamka, J. D., Vidal, D. E., & Economou-Zavlanos, N. J. (2023). Quality management systems should be implemented to close the AI translation gap and facilitate safe, ethical, and effective health AI solutions. *NPJ Digital Medicine*, 6(1), 1–5. https://doi.org /10.1038/s41746-023-00968-8

Sailesh Conjeti. PhD. (2023). Transforming healthcare: A step-by-step guide to building and deploying AI medical devices. https://www.linkedin.com/pulse/ transforming-healthcare-step-by-step-guide-building-aiconjeti

Sendak, M., Vidal, D., Trujillo, S., Singh, K., Liu, X., & Balu, S. (2023). Editorial: Surfacing best practices for AI software development and integration in healthcare. *Frontiers Research Topics*, 5. https://doi.org/10.3389/fdgth.2023.1150875

Shah, N., & Miller, K. (2022). Deploying AI in healthcare: Separating the hype from the helpful. https://hai.stanford.edu/news/deploying-ai-healthcare-separatinghype -helpful

Shakya, K. (2023). John snow labs announces turnkey deployment of medical language models as private API endpoints, boosting efficiency, security, and compliance tool to test and evaluate custom language models. https://www.johnsnowlabs.com /john-snow-labs-announces-turnkey-deployment-ofmedical-language-models-as -private-api-endpoints-boosting-efficiency-security-andcompliance/

Steidl, M., Felderer, M., & Ramler, R. (2023). The pipeline for the continuous development of artificial intelligence models—Current state of research and practice. *Journal of Systems and Software*, 199, 111615. https://doi.org/10.1016 /j.jss.2023.111615

Yarlagadda, R. T., & Research Publications. (2017). Implementation of DevOps in healthcare systems. *SSRN Electronic Journal*, 4(4), 537–541. https://doi.org/10.2139/ssrn.354372168

Zhang, A., Xing, L., Zou, J., & Wu, J. C. (2022). Shifting machine learning for healthcare from development to deployment and from models to data. *Nature Biomedical Engineering*. https://doi.org/10.1038/s41551-022-00898-y

Zinnov Content. (2024). AI in software development: revolutionizing the SDLC. https://zinnov.com/automation/ai-in-software-development-revolutionizing-the-sdlcreport/

7 AI Performance Optimization for Healthcare

Houneida Sakly, Ramzi Guetari, and Naoufel Kraiem

7.1 Introduction

7.1.1 Overview of AI Performance Optimization in Healthcare

Artificial intelligence (AI) has revolutionized the healthcare field by enabling immediate data analysis and decision-making at the point of care. Advanced technologies such as edge AI and narrow AI enable healthcare institutions to process information in close proximity, resulting in faster responses, better data protection, and increased security. Narrow AI is particularly effective in performing specific medical tasks with great competence. It is crucial to use techniques such as model compression, quantification, and pruning to optimize AI models to improve their performance while reducing complexity. The simplified use of artificial intelligence in healthcare has led to personalized treatment plans, accurate diagnostics through medical image analysis, and improved patient outcomes.

Artificial intelligence plays a key role in the detection of medical diseases, the proposal of personalized treatments, the prediction of results, the optimization of resources, the planning of employees, and the improvement of workflow efficiency and patient management. This progress highlights the potential of artificial intelligence to improve operational efficiency and foster patient-centered practices in healthcare facilities. In short, the integration of artificial intelligence technologies opens the way for significant progress in how healthcare is delivered and lived. See references: (Alowais et al., 2023; Bhagat & Kanyal, 2024; Ayuya 2024; Jordan 2023).

7.1.2 Optimizing AI Models in Healthcare Environments

Optimizing AI models in the healthcare field is essential to improve patient outcomes and operational efficiency. Techniques such as model compression, quantification, and remote computing improve the speed, accuracy, and cost-effectiveness of artificial intelligence systems. This optimization allows for rapid decision-making, which enables faster diagnostics and treatments while reducing latency and improving IT efficiency, allowing healthcare providers to provide quality service at more affordable prices. High-performance AI models facilitate real-time data analysis, improve patient follow-up,

DOI: 10.1201/9781003480594-7

and allow for personalized treatment strategies. In addition, optimization addresses scalability, ensuring accessibility across different platforms, from advanced devices to cloud servers, and promotes sustainability by reducing environmental impact. The use of optimization not only improves patient management but also promotes operational excellence and aligns with global sustainability goals. As demand for effective AI models grows in sectors such as healthcare, finance, and autonomous vehicles, it becomes essential for companies that want to fully exploit the potential of artificial intelligence. See references: (Alowais et al., 2023; Abbas, 2024; Dantas et al., 2024).

7.2   Model Compression Techniques

7.2.1   *Explanation of Model Compression*

Reducing the size of AI models in healthcare is crucial to maintain accuracy while enhancing efficiency. One effective method is the "two-way" technique, where an 8-bit model is trained with the help of two teachers through knowledge quantification and distillation. The accuracy improved by 1% to 2% compared with existing solutions, making it an ideal solution for high-end platforms. Combining different compression methods, such as pruning and deep compression quantification, has been shown to have strong potential for improving the performance of the AI model without losing accuracy. Tools such as the TensorFlow model optimization kit allow experimentation with different compression methods, thus allowing the evaluation of their effects on the overall model size, accuracy, and performance. Overall, the integration of model compression techniques is essential for optimizing AI models in healthcare environments, promoting greater efficiency while maintaining high accuracy standards (Alhussain 2024). In Table 7.1 ,we have listed various recommendations for sustainable artificial intelligence in healthcare.

7.2.2   *Benefits of Model Compression in Healthcare*

In the field of medical AI optimization, model compression methods such as pruning, quantization, and knowledge distillation offer many advantages by minimizing the size, parameters, and computational needs of AI models (Schouten et al., 2023). These methods increase the efficiency and speed of the model, making it suitable for edge computing without compromising accuracy. Han and colleagues demonstrated the effectiveness of deep compression, which combines pruning, quantization, and Huffman encoding to achieve improved results. The use of model compression approaches, such as the use of OTOV3 on ConvNeXt models, has revealed large decreases in model size, parameters, and multiple-accumulated operations (MACs) while maintaining high accuracy. The integration of OTOV3 with dynamic quantization further enhances these benefits through structuring and quantization, resulting in synergistic effects on model effectiveness. In short, model

Table 7.1 Best practice recommendations for sustainable artificial intelligence in healthcare

---

Key Points and Explanation

---

1. Eco-design and lifecycle assessment
   Conduct comprehensive lifecycle assessments to identify opportunities for eco-design, sustainable material selection, and responsible end-of-life management of AI systems in healthcare.
2. Energy-efficient AI models
   Prioritize the development of energy-efficient AI models using techniques such as model compression, quantization, and pruning to reduce energy consumption.
3. Green computing infrastructure
   Adopt green computing practices in healthcare facilities and data centers, including the use of energy-efficient hardware, optimized software, sustainable infrastructure designs, and renewable energy sources.
4. Responsible data management
   Implement efficient data compression techniques, optimize data storage systems, and regularly assess the necessity of stored data to minimize the environmental impact of AI systems.
5. Collaborative research and knowledge sharing
   Promote collaborative research efforts and knowledge sharing among healthcare institutions, AI developers, and sustainability experts to advance sustainable AI practices.
6. Continuous monitoring and improvement
   Continuously monitor and evaluate the environmental impact of AI systems in healthcare to identify areas for improvement and drive ongoing optimization.
7. Sustainable procurement and disposal practices
   Adopt sustainable procurement practices when acquiring AI hardware and components, and implement responsible disposal practices to ensure proper handling and recycling of e-waste.
8. Education and awareness
   Raise awareness about the environmental impact of AI in healthcare and the importance of sustainable practices among healthcare professionals, AI developers, and policymakers.
9. Regulatory compliance and reporting
   Ensure compliance with relevant environmental regulations and reporting requirements, conducting regular environmental impact assessments, and demonstrating adherence to sustainability standards.
10. Integration with broader sustainability initiatives
11. Integrate AI sustainability efforts with broader sustainability initiatives within healthcare organizations and society at large, aligning with institutional sustainability goals and global sustainability targets.

---

compression techniques are essential for improving the performance of AI in the healthcare field by increasing computing efficiency, enabling real-time decision-making, and reducing energy consumption. This approach is not limited to resource constraints but also helps the sustainable implementation of artificial intelligence systems in healthcare environments (Francy et al., 2024; Marinó et al., 2023).

7.2.3   Model Pruning to Reduce Complexity while Maintaining Accuracy

Pruning models is a key strategy for simplifying AI models while maintaining accuracy, particularly in the healthcare field. The combination of pruning and quantification has been shown to be effective in compressing various models, such as AlexNet, VGG-16, ResNet-18 and ResNet-50 networks, VGG, and MobileNet. This method involves the elimination of unnecessary parameters and the optimization of network structures, which considerably reduces computational complexity without sacrificing performance, as described in Figure 7.1 and Figure 7.2. Convolutional neural networks (CNNs) have achieved success across various domains, but their increased computational and storage demands pose challenges. Recent approaches aim

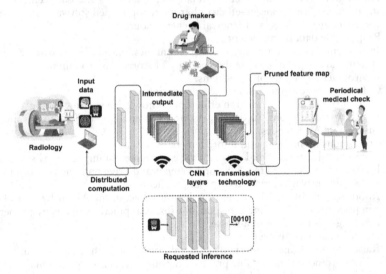

Figure 7.1 Dynamic pruning for distributed inference in a small clinic, where each inference request is pruned and distributed across multiple devices for data collection.

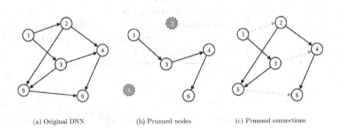

Figure 7.2 Weight pruning process in a DNN: (a) original DNN with all nodes and connections; (b) pruned nodes highlighted as nonessential; (c) pruned connections shown with dashed lines, illustrating the streamlined network structure after removing less significant weights.

to reduce these overheads through pruning and weight compression without compromising performance. This paper introduces a novel pruning criterion inspired by explainable AI (XAI), utilizing relevance scores to identify key network units. Evaluations across multiple computer vision datasets demonstrate that the method efficiently prunes CNNs, outperforming existing criteria, especially in resource-limited scenarios, and reducing computational costs while maintaining or even improving accuracy (Yeom et al., 2021).

The use of these models compressed on onboard devices has demonstrated high accuracy and fast inference times, highlighting the practical benefits of pruning techniques in situations with limited computing resources. The results highlight the importance of effective inference at the edge, which promotes faster decision-making in healthcare applications. Model pruning is essential for improving the performance of AI in healthcare by simplifying complexity while maintaining accuracy.

7.3 Quantization and Optimization Algorithms

7.3.1 *Quantization Methods for Enhancing AI Model Performance*

Quantification methods can significantly improve the performance of the AI model by reducing memory usage and computing requirements. Techniques such as post-training quantization and quantization-aware training reduce performance deterioration while achieving significant efficiency gains. For example, dynamic quantification in PyTorch resulted in a 71% decrease in model size and a 95% decrease in parameters and MACs, with an accuracy level of only 0.1%. This highlights the potential for quantification in optimizing AI models for better efficiency without sacrificing performance. In addition, the association of quantization with sparse representations, such as sparse quantization, can lead to even more pronounced efficiency improvements and advances in the development of artificial intelligence. Through the use of these new quantification methods, healthcare applications can benefit from greater model efficiency, reduced energy consumption, and faster decision-making. (Schneider-Kamp, 2021).

7.3.2 *Overview of Advanced Optimization Algorithms*

The use of advanced optimization techniques has greatly improved healthcare environments. Mixed precision training effectively reconciles accuracy and efficiency by using different numerical precisions for the components of the model, particularly in natural linguistics. Adaptive methods allow dynamic adjustments to the complexity of the model based on the characteristics of the input data, thus optimizing performance while maintaining accuracy at the same time. Automation tools such as AutoML and hyperparameter tuning simplify the development of diagrams by efficiently navigating hyperparametric spaces to achieve optimal performance with minimal manual effort. It is also essential to automate neural architecture research to create optimized architectures for specific tasks, especially in resource-constrained environments. These advances are transforming the capabilities of artificial intelligence, enabling advanced solutions to be deployed across different devices and applications. Improving model efficiency enhances performance, scalability, and durability while reducing energy consumption and overall costs (Ueda et al., 2024).

7.3.3   Application of Quantization and Optimization in Healthcare Settings

In the healthcare field, the implementation of quantification and optimization methods has a significant effect on the effectiveness of machine learning models. These methods reduce processing time while maintaining accuracy, facilitating the effective use of artificial intelligence in medical settings. Promising results have been obtained with techniques such as the QuantileTransformer, Numpy.round and KBinsDiscretizer, including the KNN and SVM models used in the Cardiovascular Disease Prediction Dataset. Quantification techniques have led to a significant reduction in temporal complexity without negatively impacting the accuracy of the model. Using Numpy.round and KBinsDiscretizer has shown improved time efficiency, which is essential for real-time applications in healthcare environments. This optimization approach not only simplifies the representation of data but also improves the responsiveness of AI models, making them more effective in critical healthcare situations. Overall, advances in quantification and optimization highlight their critical role in improving the operational efficiency of machine learning applications in the healthcare sector. See references: (Goswami et al., 2024; Abid et al., 2022, pp. 1–5).

7.4   Strategies for Efficient Inference at the Edge

7.4.1   Understanding Inference at the Edge in Healthcare Applications

Edge AI is revolutionizing healthcare by making it easier to make decisions faster and improving patient outcomes through local data manipulation. This technology allows healthcare professionals to use real-time analysis to make more accurate diagnoses and treatment plans. Improving artificial intelligence on screen involves addressing computational constraints, memory bandwidth, and power consumption on screens, especially with complex CNN models such as YOLOv8x and EfficientNet-B7, which present challenges owing to their large FLOPs and parameter requirements.

A promising solution is a hardware-software optimization framework that uses the AMD SoC-FPGA with the ZYNQ architecture and high-level synthesis (HLS) techniques. This structure improves CNN inference on remote devices by optimizing processes such as partitioning, mapping, data transfer, and the use of HLS design patterns, which allows performance criteria such as latency, throughput, and energy efficiency to be met. Several strategies, such as model splitting, runtime optimization, lightweight architecture design, and on-board device-specific enhancements, further enhance deep learning models on on-board devices. Advances such as depth-separable convolutions simplify models without sacrificing their performance. The integration of artificial intelligence with IoT and 5G technologies is also a revolution in real-time data processing in the healthcare field, leading to a better understanding of personalized and proactive support. Overall, these advances in edge AI have contributed to faster decision-making, better diagnostic accuracy, and improved patient outcomes. See references: ("Edge AI For Real-Time Inference", 2024; Alhussain, 2024, pp. 26–30).

7.4.2 Importance of Efficient Inference for Faster Decision-making

Effective decision-making in healthcare applications relies primarily on simplified inference. Processing data near its source significantly reduces latency, enabling real-time analytics that lead to rapid insights and improved patient outcomes. The fusion of artificial intelligence with the IoT and cloud computing is revolutionizing data processing, enabling healthcare providers to provide personalized assistance on the basis of the latest information. In addition, the development of advanced artificial intelligence systems in the healthcare field has solved challenges related to computing power and limited resources, resulting in improved diagnostic accuracy and treatment efficiency. Fast inference times are essential for rapid response in situations where rapid decision-making is critical to achieve optimal results. See references: ("Edge AI For Real-Time Inference", 2024; "Intel® Arc™ Graphics Empowers Medical Imaging AI Inference Solution", 2023, pp. 1–5).

7.4.3 Reducing Latency in Real-time Healthcare Scenarios through Edge Computing

Improving real-time decision-making in healthcare is critical to using advanced computing to obtain quick answers and ensure optimal operation. By processing data near its source, cloud computing reduces latency and bandwidth usage, allowing real-time AI applications to work more efficiently. The use of advanced algorithms designed for speed further improves the performance of AI models in healthcare, making it easier to transmit critical knowledge quickly. Experiments at the limit have shown that compact models can achieve high precision with minimal inference times, making them suitable for use in resource-limited environments. Performing inference tasks on remote devices reduces network latency, resulting in faster responses for applications that are sensitive to latency. Among these methods, scalability can be improved by dividing model levels or data samples among multiple devices. The integration of edge computing and AI technologies in healthcare is transforming care delivery by enabling real-time diagnoses, treatment decisions, and continuous patient monitoring. With reinforcement learning-based dynamic pruning and explainable AI, healthcare systems can process data efficiently at the edge, reducing latency and improving decision-making speed. This enhances patient management by allowing personalized care and timely interventions. Additionally, the use of AI improves operational efficiency, reducing costs through optimized workflows and resource allocation. Ultimately, these innovations lead to better patient outcomes, increased healthcare facility efficiency, and lower operational expenses, creating a more effective healthcare system (Baccour et al., 2024; Kum et al., 2022; Braunstein, 2021).

7.5 Case Studies on AI Performance Optimization in Healthcare

7.5.1 Real-world Examples of Successful AI Model Optimization

A convincing illustration of the successful improvement of the AI model in healthcare can be seen in a research project that focused on optimizing a diabetes sample from the Pima Indian community. In this study, researchers explored different optimization algorithms, such as the bird optimization algorithm and the particle society algorithm, to assess their influence on diabetes management decision-making processes. Through a thorough analysis of various techniques and indicators, such as the optimal value, mean, median, and standard deviation, the study highlighted the effectiveness of the opposite bird optimization algorithm compared with other methods. This study demonstrates the importance of artificial intelligence and metaheuristic algorithms in transforming medical diagnosis and treatment strategies, laying the foundation for future healthcare innovations. See Chatterjee et al. (2024).

7.5.2 Impact of Optimized AI Models on Patient Outcomes

Refined artificial intelligence models have a significant impact on patient outcomes in healthcare, transforming patient care through advanced algorithms and model compression techniques. These systems make it possible to personalize treatments and improve diagnostic accuracy by analyzing large numbers of samples to accurately predict patient outcomes, leading to higher cure rates and greater patient satisfaction. The inclusion of artificial intelligence in diagnostic procedures enables early detection of diseases such as cancer, guaranteeing rapid and effective treatment. In addition, AI optimization improves decision-making processes by offering real-time recommendations to healthcare professionals, accelerating the interpretation of traditional data and highlighting urgent situations. The result is shorter waiting times and better patient flow in emergency departments. Through the use of artificial intelligence-based decision support systems, practitioners can quickly make informed treatment decisions, resulting in more beneficial outcomes for patients. Advances in artificial intelligence models highlight their potential to transform patient care through personalized treatment strategies, improved diagnostic accuracy, and enhanced decision-making capability for healthcare providers. See references: (Alowais et al., 2023; Ayuya, 2024).

7.6 Challenges and Considerations for Implementing Optimization Techniques in Healthcare

7.6.1 Barriers to Implementing Optimization Techniques in Healthcare

Overcoming barriers in applying optimization techniques to healthcare is crucial to ensuring their successful integration into systems. Balancing complexity and model performance is a major issue. While advanced AI models can improve accuracy, they require significant computing resources, which can lead to longer response times that do not meet urgent medical needs. To simplify these models in terms of efficiency without sacrificing accuracy, careful consideration is necessary. Another major challenge is the lack of comprehension regarding the use of artificial intelligence in real healthcare environments. It is essential to conduct a thorough assessment of AI technologies in specific communities, especially in resource-constrained environments. There are no AI models designed for specific health challenges, such as COVID-19 detection, which highlights transparency concerns about data sources and the importance of adaptive methods. In addition, infrastructure constraints, costs, engineering difficulties, monitoring capabilities, and implementation problems can hinder the effective use of artificial healthcare optimization techniques. Achieving an optimal balance between processing speed and model accuracy is critical to improving machine learning applications in the medical field. To overcome this difficulty, it is necessary to adopt innovative preprocessing strategies, strong algorithms capable of handling different data sources, and well-planned methods to effectively implement optimized artificial intelligence models. See the following references: ("Intel® Arc™ Graphics Empowers Medical Imaging AI Inference Solution", 2023, pp. 1–5; Okolo, 2022; Dantas et al., 2024; Ayuya, 2024; Goswami et al., 2024; Abbas, 2024).

7.6.2 Ethical Considerations and Regulatory Challenges

The integration of AI in healthcare poses ethical dilemmas and regulatory challenges that are essential for responsible use. A cultural transition is needed within healthcare institutions, with a focus on effective communication, employee involvement, and a positive attitude toward technology. Clear protocols for accountability and engagement in the AI decision-making process are crucial for addressing ethical and legal complexities. In addition, obtaining informed consent from patients requires transparent discussions about the role of AI, risks, and benefits, which can help patients make decisions.

As healthcare integrates advanced technologies such as blockchain for data security and IoT with cloud computing for real-time reality, it becomes essential to consider ethical issues. While these technologies improve patient care, they also raise issues related to privacy, transparency, and data security. The importance of ethical frameworks and regulatory rules is underlined by challenges such as bias in artificial intelligence algorithms, the lack of personalized care, and the need for continuous optimization.

It is essential to take these ethical factors into account in efforts to optimize artificial intelligence to strengthen trust between the players involved while guaranteeing accountability in patient care. By proactively addressing these challenges, healthcare organizations can reconcile innovation and accountability, fully exploiting the impact of artificial intelligence on healthcare outcomes. See reference: (Bhagat & Kanyal, 2024).

7.6.3 *Overcoming Obstacles to Adoption*

In the healthcare field, various challenges need to be addressed to ensure seamless integration with existing systems. A major challenge is the lack of understanding of the functionality of artificial intelligence in real situations, especially in regions with low resources such as the Global South. It is essential to undertake a thorough assessment and evaluation of AI tools in some communities to address this issue. In addition, there is a lack of AI models designed to address urgent health needs, such as the detection of diseases like COVID-19, highlighting the importance of transparent data sources and appropriate strategies.

It is also difficult to find prospective studies that use real data in artificial intelligence analyses, which limits the flexibility of the model in less-than-ideal clinical situations. Researchers from disadvantaged countries are starting to use AI in the healthcare field, highlighting the importance of scalability and practicality for effective implementation. In addition, ethical dilemmas, regulatory barriers, and adoption barriers must be carefully addressed to ensure the responsible use of artificial intelligence in the healthcare field.

The integration of AI optimization techniques can be improved by focusing on consistency, reproducibility, scalability, and ethical principles derived from real-world situations. Addressing these challenges will result in better patient management, improved decision-making processes, and overall better health outcomes. See references: (Okolo 2022; Dantas et al., 2024; Jordan 2023).

7.7 Conclusion

7.7.1 *Recap of Key Points Discussed Regarding AI Performance Optimization in Healthcare*

Healthcare AI optimization focuses on methods such as quantification and pruning to improve computing efficiency while maintaining accuracy. Key techniques such as knowledge distillation and lightweight architectural designs offer distinct advantages for fine-tuning artificial intelligence models in clinical contexts. The use of AI can transform patient management through predictive analytics, population health management, and customized treatment methods. However, challenges such as bias and lack of personalization need to be addressed to ensure the fair and effective use of artificial intelligence in healthcare. In the future, artificial intelligence can significantly simplify management and administration in healthcare operations. Predictive analytics can predict patient admission rates, allowing for proactive adjustments in personnel and resources. In addition, artificial intelligence can help meet regular standards by constantly monitoring operations to identify risks or areas of noncompliance. The evolution of AI optimization techniques highlights their transformative role in healthcare. After artificial intelligence is integrated, the goal is to transform patient management, improve operational efficiency, and improve access to high-quality treatments. Continued exploration of these strategies will continue to drive innovations in healthcare technology. See references: (Alowais et al., 2023; Mingle, 2023; Dantas et al., 2024).

7.7.2 Future Trends and Directions for Further Research and Development

The future of optimizing AI in healthcare presents many promising perspectives, particularly with a focus on explainable AI (XAI), which enhances the transparency of algorithms, promotes trust among healthcare professionals, and improves critical decision-making. In addition, network learning is essential for preserving data confidentiality, allowing collaborative model training without disclosing sensitive patient information. The integration of predictive genetics with artificial intelligence has transformative potential for personalized medicine, thus enabling treatment strategies adapted to genetic profiles. Innovative methods such as LoRA and quantification are being implemented to improve efficiency and cost-effectiveness, leading to progress in various sectors. This will allow for greater access to advanced AI capabilities and foster technological innovation. As researchers study new compression methods and optimize models for real-time decisions, the healthcare sector can anticipate improved patient outcomes, efficiency, and service delivery. Continued investment in research, development, and education is essential to fully realize this progress. By adopting edge AI, narrow AI, model compression, and federated learning while meeting ethical standards, there is a unique opportunity to transform the delivery of care, benefiting patients, healthcare providers, and businesses. See references: (Alowais et al., 2023; Kumar et al., 2024; Jordan, 2023).

References

Abbas, A. (2024). The future of AI development: Trends in model quantization and efficiency optimization. https://www.unite.ai/the-future-of-ai-development-trends-in-model-quantization-and-efficiency-optimization/

Abid, A., Sinha, P., Harpale, A., Gichoya, J., & Purkayastha, S. (2022). Optimizing medical image classification models for edge devices. In *Distributed Computing and Artificial Intelligence, Volume 1: 18th International Conference 18* (pp. 77–87). Springer International Publishing.

Alhussain, A. (2024). Efficient processing of convolutional neural networks on the edge: A hybrid approach using hardware acceleration and dual-teacher compression. https://doi.org/10.1109/vtc2024-spring62846.2024.10683049

Alowais, S. A., Alghamdi, S. S., Alsuhebany, N., Alqahtani, T., Alshaya, A., Almohareb, S. N., Aldairem, A., Alrashed, M., Saleh, K. B., Badreldin, H. A., Yami, A., Harbi, S. A., & Albekairy, A. M. (2023). Revolutionizing healthcare: The role of artificial intelligence in clinical practice. *BMC Medical Education*, 23(1). https://doi.org/10.1186/s12909-023-04698-z

Ayuya, C. (2024). AI model optimization: 6 key techniques. https://www.eweek.com /artificial-intelligence/ai-model-optimization/

Baccour, E., Erbad, A., Mohamed, A., Hamdi, M., & Guizani, M. (2024). Reinforcement learning-based dynamic pruning for distributed inference via explainable AI in healthcare IoT systems. *Future Generation Computer Systems*, 155, 1–17. https://doi.org/10.1016/j.future.2024.01.021

Bhagat, S. V., & Kanyal, D. (2024). Navigating the future: The transformative impact of artificial intelligence on hospital management: A comprehensive review. *Cureus*, 16(2). https://doi.org/10.7759/cureus.54518

Braunstein, V. (2021). How edge computing is transforming healthcare. https:// resources.nvidia.com/en-us-healthcare-and-edge-ai/healthcare-at-the-edge

Chatterjee, R., Amir, M., Pradhan, D. K., Chakraborty, F., Kumar, M., Verma, S., Ruba Abu Khurma, & García-Arenas, M. (2024). FNN for diabetic prediction using oppositional whale optimization algorithm. *IEEE Access*, 12, 20396–20408. https://doi.org/10.1109/access.2024.3357993

Damian Mingle. (2023). Optimizing healthcare operations: AI's role in streamlining management and administration. https://medhealthoutlook.com/optimizing -healthcare-operations-ais-role-in-streamlining-management-and-administration/

Dantas, P. V., Sabino da Silva, W., Cordeiro, L. C., & Carvalho, C. B. (2024). A comprehensive review of model compression techniques in machine learning. *Applied Intelligence*, 54(22), 11804–11844. https://doi.org/10.1007/s10489-024 -05747-w

Edge Ai for Real-Time Inference. (2024). https://www.restack.io/p/real-time-ai -inference-answer-edge-ai-real-time-inference-cat-ai

Edge AI: Evaluation of Model Compression Techniques for Convolutional Neural Networks. (2024). Arxiv.org. https://arxiv.org/html/2409.02134v1

Francy, S., & Singh, R. (2024). Edge AI: Evaluation of model compression techniques for convolutional neural networks. arXiv. https://doi.org/10.48550/arXiv.2409 .02134

Goswami, M., Mohanty, S., & Pattnaik, P. M. (2024). Optimization of machine learning models through quantization and data bit reduction in healthcare datasets. *Franklin Open*, 8, 100136–100136. https://doi.org/10.1016/j.fraope .2024.100136

Intel® Arc™ Graphics Empowers Medical Imaging AI Inference Solution. (2023). https://networkbuilders.intel.com/docs/networkbuilders/intel-arc-graphics -empowers-medical-imaging-ai-inference-solution-1722407149.pdf

Jordan, J. (2023). Leveraging edge AI, narrow AI, and model compression to revolutionize healthcare: Enhancing patient care, streamlining processes, and improving. https://www.linkedin.com/pulse/leveraging-edge-ai-narrow-model-co mpression-enhancing-james-jordan

Kum, S., Oh, S., Yeom, J., & Moon, J. (2022). Optimization of Edge Resources for Deep Learning Application with Batch and Model Management. *Sensors*, 22(17), 6717. https://doi.org/10.3390/s22176717

Marinó, G., Petrini, A., Malchiodi, D., & Frasca, M. (2023). Deep neural networks compression: A comparative survey and choice recommendations.

Neurocomputing, 520, 152–170. https://doi.org/10.1016/j.neucom.2022.11.072 and cited in the section 7.2.2 Benefits of Model Compression in Healthcare

Okolo, C. T. (2022). Optimizing human-centered AI for healthcare in the Global South. *Patterns*, 100421. https://doi.org/10.1016/j.patter.2021.100421

Schneider-Kamp, A. (2021). The potential of AI in care optimization: Insights from the user-driven co-development of a care integration system. Inquiry, 58, 469580211017992. https://doi.org/10.1177/00469580211017992

Schouten, A. M., Flipse, S. M., van Nieuwenhuizen, K. E., Jansen, F. W., van der Eijk, A. C., & van den Dobbelsteen, J. J. (2023). Operating room performance optimization metrics: A systematic review. *Journal of Medical Systems*, 47(1). https://doi.org/10.1007/s10916-023-01912-9

Ueda, D., Walston, S. L., Fujita, S., Fushimi, Y., Tsuboyama, T., Kamagata, K., Yamada, A., Yanagawa, M., Ito, R., Fujima, N., Kawamura, M., Nakaura, T., Matsui, Y., Tatsugami, F., Fujioka, T., Nozaki, T., Hirata, K., & Naganawa, S. (2024). Climate change and artificial intelligence in healthcare: Review and recommendations toward a sustainable future. *Diagnostic and Interventional Imaging*. https://doi.org/10.1016/j.diii.2024.06.002

Yeom, S.-K., Seegerer, P., Lapuschkin, S., Binder, A., Wiedemann, S., Müller, K.-R., & Samek, W. (2021). Pruning by explaining: A novel criterion for deep neural network pruning. Pattern Recognition, 115, 107899. https://doi.org/10.1016/j.patcog.2021.107899

8 Scaling AI Capabilities and Establishing a Roadmap for Sustainable Growth in Healthcare

Houneida Sakly, Ramzi Guetari, and Naoufel Kraiem

8.1 Introduction

8.1.1 Background of AI in Healthcare

The healthcare field is being transformed by artificial intelligence (AI), which mimics human intelligence to analyze complex medical data. It can be used in many areas, from simplifying administrative tasks to improving clinical decision-making and personalizing treatment plans. The implementation of artificial intelligence is changing the way healthcare is delivered, manifesting itself in improved quality, efficiency, and accuracy of patient care, as shown in Figure 8.1.

By analyzing vast datasets from medical records, AI technology stands out in the prediction, diagnosis, and treatment of disease, enabling vastly improved disease diagnosis processes. Radiology is an area where AI plays an important role in the interpretation of X-rays, leading to better outcomes for patients. As AI evolves and is integrated into healthcare systems around the world, research continues to explore its potential in different medical disciplines.

However, the integration of AI into healthcare raises ethical concerns, such as data privacy issues, the risk of job displacement due to automation, and the risk of reinforcing existing prejudices. Although there are many benefits, the cautious attitudes of healthcare leaders toward new technologies pose obstacles to their widespread use.

Overall, artificial intelligence represents a significant advance in healthcare, "with the potential to improve patient outcomes and radically transform the landscape of medical practice (Bajwa et al., 2021).

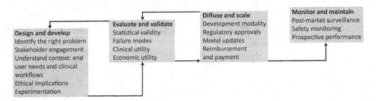

Figure 8.1 Multistep, iterative approach to build effective and reliable AI-augmented systems in healthcare.

DOI: 10.1201/9781003480594-8

8.1.2 *Importance of Scaling AI Capabilities in Healthcare*

Expanding AI capabilities in healthcare is crucial for transforming the industry and addressing longstanding challenges. The Department of Health and Human Services (HHS) views AI as essential for advancing health and wellness across America. To achieve this goal, the HHS is developing a comprehensive AI strategy that promotes familiarity and proficiency with AI technologies, encourages best practices, and accelerates the adoption of AI solutions.

Current efforts to utilize AI in healthcare face obstacles due to a lack of unified strategies and collaboration among stakeholders. Therefore, it is vital for policymakers and healthcare leaders to create a dedicated AI strategy to maximize its benefits throughout the healthcare system. This strategy should prioritize engaging the public and staff, ensuring data quality, adhering to regulatory standards, training the workforce, and addressing ethical considerations.

AI has the potential to revolutionize various aspects of healthcare beyond clinical applications, including prevention, operational efficiency, and administrative tasks. By concentrating on impactful areas, AI can drive transformative changes and enhance productivity within healthcare environments (Maleki et al., 2024).

The evolution of AI technology highlights the need for broader implementation across different healthcare stages. As solutions advance from improving routine tasks to facilitating home-based care through remote monitoring and virtual assistants, cultural shifts within organizations are essential for effective integration into clinical workflows. With advancements in deep learning and natural language processing, enhancing AI capabilities in healthcare promises significant improvements in patient outcomes and operational effectiveness. See references: (Mek, 2021, pp. 1–5; Spatharou et al., 2020; Thornton et al., 2024).

8.2 Building Robust AI Ecosystems in Healthcare

8.2.1 *Development of AI Centers of Excellence*

Establishing AI centers of excellence in healthcare requires a collaborative framework that brings together specialists from different fields to foster innovation and ethical standards. An AI council made up of specialists in data analytics, informatics, and clinical informatics is crucial to optimally benefit from AI technologies. In its Center of Excellence in Data Science and Artificial Intelligence, Intermountain Healthcare highlights this approach by combining different insights to improve patient care through the use of machine learning. To facilitate the smooth integration of AI technologies, it is necessary to focus on promoting interoperability within existing systems, including ensuring compatibility with legacy systems. Ensuring this compatibility is essential for moving to AI-based solutions without disrupting healthcare operations. In addition, enhancing the skills of healthcare professionals to facilitate the integration of AI tools into day-to-day operations is vital. Comprehensive training can help employees use AI effectively, improving their operational efficiency. By creating an atmosphere of cooperation with players in the field, hospital facilities can identify new opportunities and accelerate advances in healthcare. The open exchange of AI research, data, and models will further improve the quality of AI applications in the field. Transparent governance structures are crucial for controlling AI implementation, ensuring accountability and ethical decision-making, and guaranteeing patient safety. These approaches are essential for improving the integration of artificial intelligence into nursing and healthcare services in general. See reference: (Rowe, 2021).

8.2.2   *Adopting AI Operations (AIOps) Frameworks*

AI Operation (AIOps) frameworks can have a significant effect on IT operations and patient care in healthcare. By incorporating artificial intelligence into IT procedures, healthcare facilities can automate tasks, anticipate problems before they disrupt patient care, and optimize overall outcomes. The ability of AIOps to analyze data in real-time is a major advantage, enabling constant monitoring of healthcare systems and early detection of anomalies in patient data. Owing to this competence, healthcare service providers can quickly resolve potential problems, thereby enhancing patient safety.

Predictive maintenance of medical equipment and optimization of resources are also supported by AIOps by analyzing historical data on patient use and movement. In this proactive strategy, interruptions to care delivery are reduced, and resources are used efficiently. In addition, AIOps encourage collaboration between IT and medical staff by providing actionable information in an accessible format, enabling providers to make informed decisions that improve patient care (Ramezani et al., 2023).

Despite these benefits, challenges such as data protection concerns and regulatory compliance need to be addressed for successful implementation. AI analytics should be prioritized by healthcare organizations to ensure patient data protection and effective integration of AIOps with IT systems already in place. Overall, it is crucial for healthcare organizations to adopt AIOps frameworks to optimize their IT operations, improve patient care, and maintain their competitiveness in an ever-changing healthcare environment. See references: (Johnston, 2024; Yelne et al., 2023).

8.2.3   *Fostering Upskilling through Cross-functional Teams*

To optimize the development of healthcare skills, it is essential to consider the changing landscape impacted by the integration of artificial intelligence. It is critical that healthcare facilities place a high value on training diverse teams with medical and data science expertise to fully leverage AI technologies to improve patient care. Research by European healthcare providers and the Cleveland Clinic highlights the importance of comprehensive training programs that combine theoretical knowledge with hands-on experience in artificial intelligence tools. The creation of new functions that combine medical and data science skills underscores the importance of a culture of continuous learning and multidisciplinary cooperation. Companies must invest in improving front-line staff and implementing lifelong learning initiatives to prepare health professionals to integrate AI into their work processes. Collaborative training that involves nurses, data specialists, and AI specialists is crucial for promoting teamwork and achieving optimal patient outcomes.

In short, improving skills through the use of interdisciplinary teams in healthcare requires a collective commitment to harness artificial intelligence, improve scientific knowledge, and foster collaboration and innovation. Healthcare facilities can harness AI's transformative potential by investing in specific training programs, creating new professional roles, and forming interdisciplinary research groups. See references: (Bhagat & Kanyal, 2024; Spatharou et al., 2020; Yelne et al., 2023).

8.3 Strategic Planning for Scaling AI in Healthcare

8.3.1 Resource Allocation

Optimizing resource allocation is key to improving AI skills in healthcare, including in hospital administration. The use of artificial intelligence for predictive analytics has a disruptive impact on the effective management of resources, such as personnel, medical supplies, and facility utilization. Artificial intelligence enables healthcare organizations to make informed policy decisions by analyzing historical data as well as current trends and future projections, resulting in lower expenses, improved resource management, and increased responsiveness to changing patient demands. This proactive approach allows timely operational adjustments, minimizing waste while maximizing resource efficiency.

However, it is difficult to find a balance between the financial investments required to implement AI and other competing priorities in healthcare. Hospitals need to assess the cost-effectiveness of AI projects, ensuring that they meet strategic objectives and budget constraints. Showcasing initiatives ensures that AI efforts are aligned with the company's mission and values, facilitating seamless integration into management practices. By thoughtfully aligning resources, hospitals can maximize the use of their available resources and take full advantage of AI advances, improving the overall efficiency and quality of patient care according to a list of criteria listed in Table 8.1. See reference: (Bhagat & Kanyal, 2024).

8.3.2 Setting Measurable Milestones

It is crucial to create concrete criteria for effectively expanding AI applications in the healthcare field. With clear and achievable goals, healthcare institutions can monitor progress and ensure that their AI initiatives are on

Table 8.1 Inclusion and exclusion criteria

Criterion	Inclusion	Exclusion
Type of study	Qualitative, quantitative, mixed method, and review studies in peer-reviewed journals	Letters, comments, conference abstracts, editorials, and theses
Language	English	All other languages
Study variables	Includes (1) artificial intelligence/ machine learning and relevant terms, and (2) allocation of health care resources	Does not include (1) artificial intelligence/machine learning and relevant terms, or (2) allocation of health care resources
Study context	Health care resource allocation at either the population level or hospital level	All other resource allocation scenarios

track. It is essential to assess the readiness of current operations, identify inefficiencies that artificial intelligence can resolve, and define success through quantifiable outcomes.

By creating a roadmap with clear criteria, companies can improve their resource allocation and prioritize key areas for AI integration. This allows healthcare leaders to assess the impact of AI on revenue cycle management, patient management effectiveness, and global economies. In particular, it facilitates the monitoring of progress and allows organizations to modify their strategies based on real-time data and feedback.

In summary, establishing concrete criteria is essential for strategically planning the adoption of AI technologies in healthcare. It provides a structured framework for assessing progress, making informed decisions, and fostering sustainable growth through the integration of artificial intelligence. See references: (Thornton et al., 2024; /content/dam/advisory/en/authors/John-League, 2023; Abdelghany & Abdelmksoud, 2024; Shaikh, 2020, pp. 1–5; Yelne et al., 2023).

8.3.3 Tracking Progress

To effectively monitor the expansion of AI applications in healthcare, a strategic planning framework is essential. The proper sharing of resources ensures that funds and support are directed to the necessary AI projects. By setting measurable goals, companies can track the progress of AI implementations and adjust their strategies as needed. Regular monitoring ensures that the goals of AI integration are met while potential barriers to successful expansion are identified. Using data-driven performance indicators, companies can make informed decisions about optimizing their AI initiatives. This proactive approach allows stakeholders to quickly resolve issues, leading to continuous improvement in the application of AI technology. In summary, monitoring the expansion of AI capabilities in healthcare is critical to ensuring success and adaptability in medical environments. By establishing a strong policy framework with the precise allocation of resources and measurable goals, companies can effectively monitor progress, address challenges, and foster sustainable growth through the integration of artificial intelligence. See references: (Wu et al., 2023; Thornton et al., 2024).

8.4 Long-term Success and Adaptability in Clinical Settings

8.4.1 Establishing a Roadmap for Sustainable Growth

To foster sustainable growth in healthcare, companies must focus on establishing fundamental principles that ensure the reliability and effectiveness of AI systems. Having a strong data platform is critical, as it is the foundation for AI initiatives. Data quality is critical for generating actionable insights, and moving to cloud-based platforms can increase the growth capacity and flexibility needed for the widespread deployment of artificial intelligence. In addition, it is essential that organizations prioritize the monitoring and maintenance of AI systems after they are in place to detect risks and adverse events effectively. Collaboration among healthcare entities, regulatory authorities, and AI developers is essential for analyzing relevant data for performance assessment and risk management. Through the integration of different datasets, good management practices, and building trust in artificial intelligence solutions, healthcare organizations can fully harness the potential of artificial intelligence to transform healthcare practices. See references: (Mek, 2021, pp. 1–5; Siwicki, 2024).

8.4.2 Ensuring Adaptability to Changing Healthcare Landscape

To adapt effectively to the changing healthcare landscape, companies must leverage technology and AI. The NHS in the UK is facing new demands from an aging population and staff shortages, highlighting the importance of integrating artificial intelligence to improve the quality of care and productivity. It is essential to adopt a comprehensive strategy to expand the use of artificial intelligence on a large scale across the NHS to ensure large-scale benefits. The integration of AI takes place in three stages. The first step focuses on automating routine administrative tasks to improve operational efficiency. The second step is moving toward home care through remote monitoring and virtual assistants, allowing patients to actively manage their health. There has also been an increase in the use of artificial intelligence in various medical fields, such as oncology and cardiology. Defining strategic priorities for investment in AI in healthcare and implementing uniform data regulatory standards are key to supporting a cost-effective expansion of artificial intelligence solutions. Setting standards for data sharing will foster confidence in new AI technologies among patients and healthcare providers. In addition, the creation of centers of excellence dedicated to artificial intelligence can bring together expertise and accelerate the implementation of advanced skills within national healthcare systems. Successful future healthcare will be based on the harmonization of human knowledge with artificial intelligence innovation, ensuring a balance between technological progress and compassionate patient care. By adopting responsible approaches to the integration of artificial intelligence, healthcare companies can better adapt to new trends and meet challenges in the ever-changing world of health. See references: (Spatharou et al., 2020; Thornton et al., 2024).

8.5   Case Studies: Successful Implementation of AI in Healthcare

Artificial intelligence (AI) is making significant progress in the healthcare field, as evidenced by its successful implementation through various institutions. An outstanding example is the collaboration between Cleveland Clinic and IBM, where artificial intelligence has revolutionized personalized healthcare plans. Through the analysis of large databases, the clinic customizes strategies to meet each patient's specific needs, which improves the accuracy and results of therapy.

Ciox Health in Georgia has also adopted artificial intelligence to improve medical data management and work processes. Using machine learning, Ciox Health simplifies access to clinical data, enhancing the accuracy and efficiency of information flow within the healthcare system. This ensures rapid access to critical data, facilitating informed decision-making and optimizing healthcare workflows.

The Johns Hopkins Hospital in Maryland has partnered with GE to implement predictive AI techniques that improve the effectiveness of hospital visits. This implementation has reduced wait times and optimized resources, resulting in increased patient satisfaction. The integration of predictive intelligence illustrates how technology can lead to real-world improvements in healthcare operations.

This highlights the transformative impact of AI in healthcare through its personalization of planning, effective workflow management, and predictive capabilities. The successes of these institutions are valuable examples for the healthcare sector as a whole, demonstrating effective AI integration that improves patient management and operational excellence. See references: (Bhagat & Kanyal, 2024; Yelne et al., 2023).

8.6   Challenges and Risks Associated with Scaling AI in Healthcare

8.6.1   Data Privacy and Security Concerns

Protecting patient privacy and ensuring data security are crucial when integrating artificial intelligence into healthcare systems. It is essential to have strong security measures in place and to carefully manage artificial intelligence solutions while respecting ethical considerations. Promoting justice, transparency, and accountability to reduce healthcare inequalities and ensure the responsible use of AI. A variety of artificial intelligence algorithms is essential to building trust between healthcare providers and patients.

It is essential to create engagement frameworks to clarify responsibility for AI-influenced decisions that impact patient care, taking into account legal, ethical, and medical issues. It is crucial to conduct regular audits of artificial intelligence systems to detect biases, disparities, and ethical issues that may arise during decision-making processes. By proactively addressing the challenges of data privacy and security, healthcare organizations can use AI in an ethical and responsible way, resulting in improved patient management outcomes. See references: (Mek, 2021, pp. 6–8; Siwicki, 2024; Yelne et al., 2023).

8.6.2   *Regulatory Compliance Issues*

While respecting regular standards, it is essential to integrate artificial intelligence solutions in the healthcare field. The complex legal landscape of the healthcare sector, highlighted by laws such as HIPAA in the US, represents a major challenge for organizations that want to adopt innovations in artificial intelligence. Ensuring that the implementation of artificial intelligence complies with legal requirements, preserves patient privacy, and preserves data security is crucial but difficult. Working with legal and compliance experts is essential to effectively align AI solutions with regulations. This process may require extensive risk assessments, data security audits, and ongoing monitoring to ensure compliance while harnessing the benefits of artificial intelligence technologies. See references: ("Artificial Intelligence in Healthcare", 2024; Yelne et al., 2023).

8.7   Future Trends and Innovations in AI for Healthcare

8.7.1   *Predictive Analytics for Personalized Medicine*

The healthcare landscape is changing with the evolution of predictive analytics, which allows providers to anticipate patient outcomes with remarkable accuracy. When artificial intelligence is used to analyze medical data such as vital signs, medical histories, and environmental factors continuously, predictive analytics can anticipate health events such as illness or hospitalization. This proactive approach enables healthcare professionals to take preventive measures, leading to better health management, fewer hospital admissions, and an improved quality of life for patients. In addition, healthcare companies benefit from better allocation of resources and delivery of care through knowledge gained from predictive analytics. The integration of AI in this area is fostering a broader shift toward personalized and proactive healthcare interventions. A large sample size allows providers to identify subtle patterns, which facilitates the creation of customized treatment plans tailored to each patient's specific needs. This method not only improves the effectiveness of management but also promotes a more patient-centered and accurate healthcare experience. The future of predictive analytics in personalized medicine promises great advances in patient management. Through continued advances in artificial intelligence and emotional intelligence, predictive analytics are designed to improve health outcomes, increase profitability, and improve the overall quality of care in the healthcare system. See reference: (Yelne et al., 2023).

8.7.2   *Integration of AI with the Internet of Medical Things (IoMT)*

The integration of artificial intelligence with the Internet of Medical Things (IoMT) is intended to transform healthcare delivery by using data from IoT devices and connected devices. This collaboration enables real-time health monitoring and personalized information for patients and healthcare professionals, facilitating early detection of health problems, ongoing management of chronic diseases, and personalized healthcare recommendations. In addition, AI has the ability to analyze genetic data to identify disease indicators and propose customized treatment plans, which reinforces precision medical strategies. This synergy not only helps healthcare professionals make informed decisions but also enables patients to play an active role in the management of their health. Furthermore, the integration of blockchain technology with artificial intelligence significantly improves the security and confidentiality of medical data in decentralized health systems. AI has the ability to monitor and protect medical information effectively on blockchain platforms, ensuring the reliability and integrity of these systems. This combination promotes the confidentiality, accuracy, and security of medical exchanges, which are essential elements of contemporary healthcare ecosystems. Overall, the combination of artificial intelligence and IoMT offers great opportunities to transform healthcare practices through the personalization of medicine, robust data protection measures, and a focus on patient management. See reference: (Yelne et al., 2023).

8.8   Conclusion

The integration of artificial intelligence (AI) into healthcare offers transformative opportunities, enabling personalized care, improving diagnostic accuracy, and encouraging medical research. However, as the field evolves, it is essential to address ethical challenges, data privacy concerns, and algorithmic biases. Maximizing the impact of artificial intelligence requires interdisciplinary collaboration, ethical standards, and attention to patient-centered approaches. By fostering a creative environment and focusing on patient rights, the potential of artificial intelligence to improve healthcare outcomes can be fully realized. Future benefits include AI-based diagnostics, prognostic analyses, and personalized treatment plans that could significantly improve patient management. Ongoing research and collaborative initiatives will be critical to ensuring that artificial intelligence works as a complement to human healthcare providers. The objective of this integration is to improve accessibility and overall quality of care, paving the way for innovative solutions in healthcare. See references: (Spatharou et al., 2020; Davenport & Kalakota, 2019; Yelne et al., 2023).

References

/content/dam/advisory/en/authors/John-League./content/dam/advisory/en/authors/Ty -Aderhold. (2023). The best AI strategy is not about AI. https://www.advisory .com/topics/artificial-intelligence/2023/09/ai-strategy

Abdelghany, M., & Abdelmksoud, M. G. (2024). GenAI for AIOps catapults digital transformation in healthcare. https://www.linkedin.com/posts/ mohaymenabdelghany_council-post-genai-for-aiops-catapults-digital-activity -7213104265030955009-HqAq

Artificial intelligence in healthcare. (2024). https://en.wikipedia.org/wiki/Artificial _intelligence_in_healthcare

Bajwa, J., Munir, U., Nori, A., & Williams, B. (2021). Artificial intelligence in healthcare: Transforming the practice of medicine. *Future Healthcare Journal*, 8(2), e188–e194. https://doi.org/10.7861/fhj.2021-0095

Bhagat, S. V., & Kanyal, D. (2024). Navigating the future: The transformative impact of artificial intelligence on hospital management: A comprehensive review. *Cureus*, 16(2). https://doi.org/10.7759/cureus.54518

Davenport, T., & Kalakota, R. (2019). The potential for artificial intelligence in healthcare. *Future Healthcare Journal*, 6(2), 94–98. https://doi.org/10.7861/ futurehosp.6-2-94

Johnston, M. A. (2024). The future of healthcare IT: How AIOps is revolutionizing patient care. https://www.linkedin.com/pulse/future-healthcare-how-aiops -revolutionizing-patient-care-johnston-8sgmc

Maleki Varnosfaderani, S., & Forouzanfar, M. (2024). The role of AI in hospitals and clinics: Transforming healthcare in the 21st century. Bioengineering (Basel), 11(4), 337. https://doi.org/10.3390/bioengineering11040337

Mek, O. (2021). U.S. department of health and human services artificial intelligence (AI) strategy. https://www.hhs.gov/sites/default/files/hhs-ai-strategy.pdf

Ramezani, M., Takian, A., Bakhtiari, A., Rabiee, H. R., Fazaeli, A. A., & Sazgarnejad, S. (2023). The application of artificial intelligence in health financing: A scoping review. *Cost Effectiveness and Resource Allocation*, 21(1). https://doi.org/10.1186 /s12962-023-00492-2

Rowe, J. (2021). Intermountain unveils AI center for excellence. https://www .healthcareitnews.com/ai-powered-healthcare/intermountain-unveils-ai-center -excellence

Shaikh, S. J. (2020). Artificial intelligence and resource allocation in healthcare: The process-outcome divide in perspectives on moral decision-making. In AI4SG@ AAAI Fall Symposium.

Siwicki, B. (2024). Cleveland Clinic's advice for AI success: Democratizing innovation, upskilling talent and more. https://www.healthcareitnews.com/news/cleveland -clinics-advice-ai-success-democratizing-innovation-upskilling-talent-and-more

Spatharou, A., Hieronimus, S., & Jenkins, J. (2020). Transforming healthcare with AI: The impact on the workforce and organizations. https://www.mckinsey.com/ industries/healthcare/our-insights/transforming-healthcare-with-ai

Thornton, N., Hardie, T., Horton, T., & Gerhold, M. (2024). Priorities for an AI in health care strategy. https://www.health.org.uk/publications/long-reads/priorities -for-an-ai-in-health-care-strategy

Wu, H., Lu, X., & Wang, H. (2023). The application of artificial intelligence in health care resource allocation before and during the COVID-19 pandemic: Scoping review. *JMIR AI*, 2, e38397. https://doi.org/10.2196/38397

Yelne, S., Chaudhary, M., Dod, K., Sayyad, A., & Sharma, R. (2023). Harnessing the power of AI: A comprehensive review of its impact and challenges in nursing science and healthcare. *Cureus*, 15(11). https://doi.org/10.7759/cureus.49252

9 Governance, Lessons, and Future Trends for Scalable AI in Healthcare

Houneida Sakly, Ramzi Guetari, Naoufel Kraiem, and Mourad Said

9.1 Introduction

9.1.1 Overview of AI in Healthcare

The integration of artificial intelligence (AI) into healthcare has increased, offering many opportunities to improve health outcomes, operational efficiency, and patient management quality. Advanced tools are designed to improve patients' journeys and expand access to healthcare globally, in line with the UN's sustainable development goals.

The applications of AI in healthcare are diverse and include the coordination of care, analysis of medical images, discovery of drugs, prediction of liver disease, cancer research and management, precision medicine, AI-based diagnostics, and health monitoring. These examples demonstrate the transformative impact of artificial intelligence on healthcare delivery.

IBM Corporation and Flatiron Health have been instrumental in the commercialization of artificial intelligence for medical analysis. In addition, large companies such as Oracle Corporation and Google Inc. are investing in cloud-based platforms designed for medical data analytics. Young startups also make a significant contribution by offering innovative and technology-oriented solutions for medical analysis.

Overall, artificial intelligence in health is leading to great advances in patient management and medical diagnostics and treatments. Using sophisticated computational algorithms and cutting-edge technologies such as quantum computing, the healthcare sector can look forward to a future filled with adaptive artificial intelligence solutions that emphasize scalability, safety, and sustainability in their implementation. See references: (Bouderhem, 2024; Dash et al., 2019).

9.1.2 Ethical Considerations

The ethical implications of artificial intelligence in healthcare are essential for influencing future patient management. As artificial intelligence advances, it is crucial to address the ethical and regulatory challenges that arise from its integration into healthcare systems. While the study of artificial intelligence

DOI: 10.1201/9781003480594-9

shows promising prospects for improving medical procedures and patient outcomes, its application poses serious challenges that require careful ethical assessment, both legal and regulatory.

A strong governance structure is essential for the effective integration of AI into healthcare practices. A thorough understanding of the ethical and regulatory issues related to the use of AI is essential. It is essential to pay particular attention to the challenges of data privacy and regulatory compliance to preserve patient information and maintain healthcare standards (Farhud et al., 2021).

While AI technologies can disrupt support for healthcare decisions, it is essential to consider the associated ethical considerations. The emphasis on patient safety, privacy, and enforcement highlights the importance of an ethical framework from the beginning of AI use.

By carefully examining these ethical and regulatory challenges, stakeholders can foster responsible growth and the effective implementation of innovative AI systems in healthcare. By addressing these issues in depth, we can not only improve health outcomes but also ensure that the benefits of artificial intelligence are realized without sacrificing ethical principles or regulatory compliance. See reference: (Mennella et al., 2024).

9.2   Ethical Considerations

9.2.1   Data Privacy Challenges

Ensuring data confidentiality is critical when integrating artificial intelligence (AI) into healthcare systems, especially as patient information becomes increasingly digital. Preserving patients' privacy rights while using AI is essential. Artificial intelligence technologies such as machine learning and deep learning rely on user data to make predictions, which requires a careful balance between accessibility and data protection.

Essential strategies such as homomorphic encryption (HE) and multiparty secure computing (SMPC) play crucial roles in preserving patient privacy and confidentiality in data-driven healthcare environments. Transparent communication and structured assessments of AI models are also essential for building trust and ensuring ethical applications in medicine. Addressing cybersecurity issues is crucial to ensuring patient safety and preserving data integrity, which leads to the implementation of security (Table 9.1) measures such as secure enclaves to address cyber threats.

The attribution of responsibility for AI results poses challenges, leading to a shift from traditional data management to a data management approach that is based on accountability and privacy. It is also crucial to reduce biases in artificial intelligence algorithms and data collection procedures to avoid exacerbating healthcare disparities. The use of convolutional neural networks (CNNs) can improve data quality by providing a holistic view of patient information, which improves the accuracy of AI-generated insights.

Table 9.1 Measures to ensure the privacy and security of personal health data

---

Potential Measures and Safeguards for Effective Data Protection

---

1. Educate healthcare personnel
2. Conduct routine risk assessment
3. Secure data with a VPN
4. Restrict access to data
5. Implement role-based access
6. Two-factor authentication
7. Encryption
8. Security awareness training

Preserving patient privacy in artificial intelligence-driven healthcare requires a multidisciplinary approach that combines technological solutions with ethical considerations. By taking strong privacy protections, promoting transparency, addressing bias, and focusing on data quality, healthcare organizations can fully exploit the potential of artificial intelligence while ensuring ethical and equitable outcomes. See references: (Wang et al., 2022; Jeyaraman et al., 2023).

9.2.1 Regulatory Compliance

Compliance with regulatory requirements is essential for integrating artificial intelligence into healthcare, with a focus on ethical standards and patient welfare. The lack of comprehensive regulations governing the use of artificial intelligence in mental health poses serious challenges. The FDA has begun overseeing artificial intelligence-based medical devices in this field, highlighting the importance of providing clear guidelines for safety and efficacy. The aim of global initiatives is to standardize regulatory approaches to artificial intelligence in healthcare, encouraging common principles that promote the responsible use of artificial intelligence in mental health treatments.

The rapid development of artificial intelligence tools in healthcare has led to numerous applications that have often not received formal validation, highlighting ethical and legal issues. Addressing these challenges is essential to ensure the ethical advancement and effective implementation of AI-based innovations in the sector. The integration of artificial intelligence raises issues related to patient privacy, well-being, and compliance with existing healthcare standards, highlighting the importance of robust regulatory frameworks (Overgaard et al., 2023).

To establish and implement ethical and regular guidelines for the integration of artificial intelligence in healthcare, it is essential to work together among policymakers, healthcare institutions, and technology specialists. These frameworks are expected to provide guidance on ethical practices, data protection, transparency, and the application of regulations such as GDPR and HIPAA. By establishing clear guidelines and benchmarks, stakeholders can strengthen their confidence in AI-enhanced healthcare solutions while focusing on safeguarding patient welfare and establishing fair treatment, as described in Table 9.2, and the different levels of risk posed by AI in healthcare systems, as shown in Table 9.3.

Translated with DeepL.com (free version). See references: (Olawade et al., 2024; Yelne et al., 2023; Dhirani et al., 2023; Bouderhem, 2024; Mennella et al., 2024).

Table 9.2 Solutions to adequately regulate the use of AI in healthcare

Potential Solutions to Adequately Regulate AI Systems
1. Establishing legally binding rules and standards under the WHO
2. Strengthening regulatory oversight
3. Promoting transparency and accountability
4. Encouraging industry self-regulation
5. Fostering international cooperation
6. Ethics in using personal health data
7. Establishing an 'AI culture' involving all stakeholders

Table 9.3 Different levels of risk posed by AI systems under the AI Act

Levels of Risks under the AI Act
1. Unacceptable risk: Such AI systems will be banned (cognitive, behavioral manipulation, social scoring, facial recognition, for instance).
2. High risk: AI systems affecting negatively safety or some fundamental rights. a) AI systems utilized in items governed by European product safety legislation. This encompasses toys, airplanes, automobiles, medical apparatuses, and elevators.. b) AI systems falling into specific areas that will have to be registered in an EU database (e.g., education, critical infrastructure, law enforcement...). All these AI systems will be assessed by relevant authorities and watchdogs before and during their lifetime.
3. General purpose and generative AI (Dwivedi et al., 2023). Such AI systems have to comply with transparency requirements. a) Obligation to disclose the fact that the content was generated by AI. b) Obligation to design the model to prevent it from generating illegal content. c) Obligation to publish summaries of copyrighted data used for training. The European Commission will evaluate the risks posed by powerful models such as GPT-4 developed by OpenAI.
4. Limited risk: Limited risk AI systems should comply with minimal transparency requirements that would allow users to make informed decisions.

9.3 Ethics and Lessons

The integration of artificial intelligence in healthcare has profoundly transformed the sector, highlighting its capabilities through various success stories. A notable example is in the field of diagnostic imaging, where advanced algorithms analyze X-rays, MRIs, and CT scans to detect subtle anomalies, improving diagnostic accuracy. AI has had a notable impact on the field of mammography, facilitating the early detection of breast cancer and improving treatment outcomes. By simplifying the analysis of medical images, artificial intelligence helps healthcare professionals provide more accurate diagnoses, which in turn improves the quality of patient care.

Another major development involves the creation of personalized treatment plans using AI. By analyzing data from genetic profiles and lifestyle factors, artificial intelligence can be used to design personalized regimens tailored to each patient. This approach improves both management efficiency and side effects while enhancing overall patient outcomes. The ability of artificial intelligence to efficiently process large datasets enables the development of strategies that consider the specific characteristics and needs of each patient (Gerke et al., 2020).

This succession highlights the potential of artificial intelligence to transform healthcare delivery by improving diagnostic accuracy and enabling personalized treatments. However, it is vital to consider ethical issues such as data protection and algorithmic bias to ensure the responsible and fair use of artificial intelligence in healthcare environments. By carefully managing these challenges and harnessing the strategic advantages of artificial intelligence, the healthcare sector can take full advantage of the transformative power of this technology to improve patient care and outcomes. See references: (Oluwafemidiakhoa, 2024; Yelne et al., 2023).

The use of artificial intelligence algorithms in healthcare faces many challenges, not least the possibility of misuse leading to misdiagnosis. A case study highlighted the ethical issues associated with artificial intelligence in medical contexts, emphasizing the importance of data accuracy and algorithmic biases. In particular, it looks at IBM's oncology system, which has been reported to provide erroneous recommendations for treating cancer on the basis of fictitious situations rather than real patient data. The difference between training data and actual healthcare situations seriously compromises the accuracy of the algorithm, highlighting a fundamental flaw in the system.

The consequences of this misuse are profound, presenting serious dangers for patients who rely on artificial intelligence for diagnosis and treatment. The case study highlighted the crucial importance of providing high-quality data and independent algorithms to ensure the reliability and effectiveness of artificial intelligence systems in healthcare. Addressing these challenges is crucial for avoiding misdiagnosis and safeguarding patient welfare, highlighting the critical importance of ethical considerations in the application of artificial intelligence technologies.

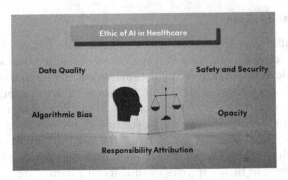

Figure 9.1 The ethic of AI in healthcare systems and healthcare organizations—legal challenges, medical information, operational efficiency, patient data, data privacy, or other ethical issues.

Key findings highlight the importance of transparent verification procedures for artificial intelligence models, clear regulatory frameworks, and ongoing research and development. By focusing on ethical standards and patient safety, healthcare professionals can reduce the risks associated with AI use and enhance the credibility of AI medical systems. Moving forward, proactive steps are essential to address these challenges to take full advantage of AI technology while ensuring positive patient outcomes. See references: ("The Future of AI in Healthcare—Treatment, Diagnostics, Ethics (Figure 9.1), Challenges in Software Development", 2024; Mennella et al., 2024).

9.4   Emerging Technologies

9.4.1   *Quantum Computing and Its Implications in Healthcare AI*

In healthcare, the combination of quantum computing and artificial intelligence (AI) has considerable potential, enabling advances such as faster diagnosis, personalized treatments, and the creation of innovative medicines. However, this integration raises ethical and regulatory issues that need to be resolved. Safeguarding patient data, preserving privacy, and reducing bias in AI algorithms are key concerns, requiring particular attention as these technologies progress. In addition, the significant expense and complexity associated with quantum computing resources hinder their widespread use in healthcare.

Collaboration among technology companies, medical institutions, and academic organizations is crucial to promoting innovation and implementing practical solutions in healthcare. For development, continued investment in research and development will be essential, as will educational programs to train a skilled workforce capable of bringing these fields closer together.

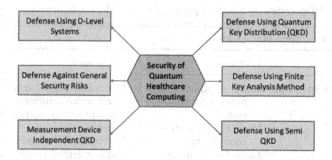

Figure 9.2 Classification of essential technologies that can guarantee security for healthcare information processing through quantum computing.

Current successful applications highlight the transformative influence of quantum computing and artificial intelligence on healthcare. Advances in MRI analysis, personalized cancer treatments, and accelerated drug discovery have led to improvements in diagnostic accuracy, personalized treatment strategies, and accelerated therapeutic developments. Although data protection and regulatory compliance are current challenges, the advances to date point to a promising future for these cutting-edge technologies in medicine.

Going forward, it is important to focus on creating adaptable AI solutions that can be scaled up efficiently while maintaining safety and sustainability. By overcoming adoption challenges, key players in healthcare can fully exploit the potential of quantum computing (Figure 9.2) and AI, transform healthcare practices, improve patient outcomes, and operational efficiency, as described in Table 9.4. See references: (Oluwafemidiakhoa, 2024; Yelne et al., 2023).

9.4.2   Other Relevant Technologies in the Healthcare Sector

The incorporation of artificial intelligence (AI) into new advances in healthcare, such as prognostic analytics and telehealth, has led to significant progress in the field. Health monitoring is enhanced by essential technologies such as the Internet of Things (IoT) and wearable devices, which offer real-time data on measurements such as heart rate and blood pressure. This combination makes it easier to detect health problems early, make personalized health recommendations, and improve overall outcomes for patients and providers.

The use of blockchain technology is also essential for enhancing data security in healthcare systems. By using artificial intelligence to manage patient medical information stored in decentralized registries, blockchain guarantees data confidentiality and security, providing secure storage and sharing of sensitive medical information while preventing unauthorized access. This partnership strengthens data protection, patient privacy, and the secure

Table 9.4 An overview of essential prerequisites for the implementation of quantum computing in healthcare service delivery, including various problems and corresponding solutions.

Requirements	Challenges	Solutions
Computational power	Lower computational power of traditional systems. Higher computational complexity. Large problem sizes. Complex system implementation.	Multidimensional spaces of quantum computers. Efficient representation of larger problems. Quantum wave interference. Unprecedented speed of quantum computing.
High-speed connectivity (5G/6G networks)	Lack of security in high-speed connectivity. Lack of scalability in quantum computers. Lack of confidentiality in information processing.	Quantum walks-based universal computing model. Inherent cryptographic features of quantum computing. Cryptographic protocols. Quantum-computing-based authentication.
Higher-dimensional quantum computing	Growing number of quantum states. Lower capacity in traditional systems. Increased processing requirements.	Increased noise resilience. Quantum channel implementation. Parallel execution of tasks.
Scalability of quantum computing	Lack of scalability in quantum computations. Lack of reusability. Lack of support for growing amount of processing. Lack of emulation environments.	Transfer learning methods. Use of neural Boltzmann machines. Physics-inspired transfer-learning protocols. FPGA-based quantum computing applications.
Fault tolerance	Lack of fault tolerance. Quantum entangled states. Errors in qubits. Lack of quantum correction code.	Monitoring qubits using ancillary qubit. Logical errors detection. Limiting error propagation.
Quantum availability of the healthcare systems	Far-away processing systems. Errors in the communication systems. Lack of computing infrastructure. Lack of service distribution.	Communication infrastructure improvement. Fault correction mechanisms Development of quantum services. Improvement in traditional computing systems.

(*Continued*)

Table 9.4 (*Continued*)

Requirements	Challenges	Solutions
Deployment of quantum gates	No cloning restriction. Challenges with coupling topology. Combinatorial optimization problems. Lack of error correction code.	Use of gate-model quantum computers. Programming gated models. Performance of factorization process.
Use of distributed topologies	Physical distances among quantum states. Latency on quantum bus execution. Requirement of coordinated infrastructure. Lack of system area network.	Development of distributed quantum technologies. Efficient quantum bus implementation. Feed-forward quantum neural networks. Dipole–dipole interaction.
Requirements for physical implementation	Higher implementation cost. Lack of resources and expertise. Lower initial revenue	Physical systems development. Cost-effective solutions. Manpower training.
Quantum ML	Extended execution time. Lack of resources and higher complexity. More implementation overhead.	Quantum-computing-based solutions. Lower computational complexity. Higher responsiveness.

exchange of healthcare data, all of which are essential in today's healthcare environment.

Furthermore, genomic medicine is an innovative application of artificial intelligence, offering customized healthcare on the basis of genetic profiles. Owing to genomic analysis based on artificial intelligence, it is possible to effectively identify genetic risks, signs of disease, and treatments tailored to an individual's genetic make-up. This has significant implications for cancer treatment, the diagnosis of rare diseases, and drug discovery, as it speeds up the analysis of large genomic datasets and supports precise therapeutic choices (Li et al., 2022).

Overall, the fusion of artificial intelligence with IoT devices, blockchain technology for data security, and advances in genomic medicine highlights the potential for renewing healthcare delivery. By harnessing these technologies effectively while taking ethical considerations into account, the future of healthcare is poised to welcome more individualized care strategies that lead to improved patient outcomes. See references: (Dhirani et al., 2023; Yelne et al., 2023).

9.5 Future Trends and Strategies

9.5.1 *Building Adaptable AI Solutions for Scalability*

Designing flexible AI solutions for scalability is essential in healthcare, where combining AI with IoT devices and wearable technology enables real-time health monitoring. By analyzing data such as heart rate and blood pressure, this capability enables early detection of health problems and provides personalized recommendations, allowing healthcare professionals to make informed decisions. In addition, blockchain enhances data protection in healthcare systems by preventing unauthorized access and modification while promoting trust and confidentiality. In genomic medicine, artificial intelligence plays a crucial role in creating tailored treatment strategies based on a person's genetic make-up, which is particularly beneficial for cancer treatment and drug discovery. To use AI tools ethically, it is essential that nursing education evolve to include courses on AI and offer continuing education opportunities to keep nurses up to date with the latest applications. Nursing student training can be enhanced with AI-powered personalized learning tools, preparing them to work collaboratively with AI in clinical situations. The fusion of quantum computing and artificial intelligence in healthcare raises serious ethical concerns about data security and patient confidentiality. Meeting infrastructure requirements, such as setting up specialized environments for quantum computers, is crucial to taking full advantage of this integration. A skilled workforce that combines quantum computing, artificial intelligence, and healthcare to design innovative solutions to complex medical challenges is crucial.

Inclusion and equity are key principles guiding the progress of AI technologies in healthcare, ensuring broad accessibility regardless of individual characteristics. Transparent evaluation processes tailored to specific contexts are essential to guarantee the reliability and cooperation of AI systems. It is essential that stakeholders work together to create ethical standards for the use of AI in the field of data security. Innovation at the intersection of quantum computing and AI in healthcare is fostered by collaborations among technology companies, healthcare institutions, and academic organizations. To drive this integration forward, continued investment in research and training programs will be essential, ultimately leading to improved patient outcomes. See references: (Oluwafemidiakhoa, 2024; Mennella et al., 2024; Yelne et al., 2023).

9.5.2 *Ensuring Security and Sustainability in AI Implementation*

Ensuring safety and sustainability is crucial when implementing AI in healthcare. The incorporation of AI technologies has many benefits, such as improved patient care and more efficient processes. However, it also raises concerns about data privacy, IT security, and ethical issues. Companies must implement rigorous data protection measures, such as encryption, access control, secure storage, and secure transmission, to keep patient data safe. Compliance with regulations such as HIPAA is essential to preserve the confidentiality of patient data.

It is crucial that algorithms are transparent to enable healthcare professionals and patients to understand the recommendations made by AI. Designing AI models that can be interpreted and explained encourages trust and responsibility in the healthcare decision-making process. Guidelines to promote equity are needed to manage biases in AI algorithms that can cause inequalities in healthcare outcomes.

Promoting standardized methods for data collection improves the quality and consistency of healthcare information used by AI systems. Standardization ensures the compatibility, reliability, and improved performance of artificial intelligence algorithms. By focusing on privacy preservation, transparency, fairness, and standardized data collection methods, companies can improve healthcare quality while preserving ethical principles, as shown in Table 9.5. See references: (Rasool et al., 2023; Yelne et al., 2023).

9.6 Adoption Challenges and Recommendations

The transition to artificial intelligence (AI) in healthcare poses several challenges that must be overcome to succeed. One of the main concerns is obtaining patients' informed consent for the use of AI-enabled services. Importantly, patients must understand the implications of AI technologies because of the complexity of the algorithms and the large datasets associated with them. It is important for healthcare providers to place great emphasis on patient awareness and transparent communication to build trust and guarantee patient autonomy.

It is equally crucial to implement accountability in AI decision-making processes. Clear guidelines must be established to determine who is responsible for the choices made by AI systems that impact patient care. It is essential that healthcare professionals, developers, and organizations share responsibility in ensuring that errors or biases in AI results are corrected. By creating accountability frameworks, it will be possible to address the legal, ethical, and medical issues associated with liability effectively.

Regular audits of AI systems are essential for identifying biases and ethical issues in decision-making processes. Healthcare institutions must invest

Table 9.5 Themes for ethical and responsible AI based on the WHO's core principles.

Themes for Ethical and Responsible AI Systems
1. Compliance with guiding principles
2. Balance innovation and responsibility
3. Engage in collaboration and dialog
4. Build organizational awareness and culture
5. Use appropriate tools and methods

in specialized teams or interdisciplinary committees to continuously monitor AI algorithms, ensuring that fairness, integrity, and compliance with ethical standards are assured. To ensure the reliability of AI systems and guarantee unbiased care for all patients, it is essential to conduct consistent evaluations.

In addition, providing comprehensive training for healthcare professionals on the fundamental concepts of artificial intelligence, data analysis, and the ethical issues involved in reducing bias and protecting data is vital. In education programs for nurses and doctors, incorporating AI training will enable professionals to acquire the skills required to use these technologies responsibly, ultimately improving patient care.

In short, resolving the future challenges of informed consent described in Figure 9.3, establishing accountability, implementing regular audits, and providing appropriate training for healthcare professionals are crucial steps to effectively integrate ethical AI into healthcare governance, as shown in Figure 9.4. See reference: (Yelne et al., 2023).

Figure 9.3 Future of AI in healthcare, patient data, and challenges to healthcare professionals.

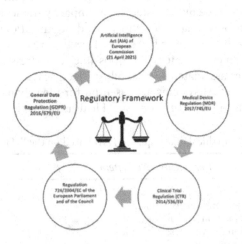

Figure 9.4 Promoting key European acts to govern AI in healthcare.

9.7 Conclusion

The incorporation of artificial intelligence into healthcare has considerable potential to improve patient care and services. Ethical principles such as transparency, fairness, and patient welfare are essential to ensure a positive impact. Building trust through clear communication, explainable algorithms, and user-centered design is crucial to ensure social acceptance of AI technologies in this field. Ethical marketing practices that match societal expectations can prevent misrepresentations of artificial intelligence capabilities.

AI and robotics have significant social implications in healthcare, offering improvements in access and equity while highlighting challenges related to bias and trust. Establishing sound ethical frameworks to guide the development and deployment of these technologies will ensure that their benefits extend to all individuals, regardless of socioeconomic status or geographical location.

It is crucial that stakeholders constantly reflect, adapt, and collaborate to address the ethical complexities associated with AI in healthcare. Collaboration among policymakers, developers, healthcare providers, and patients is essential to address issues such as data privacy, regulatory compliance, and bias in algorithms. A focus on patient welfare, equity, and accountability is essential for using AI technologies responsibly.

Future developments, such as advances in quantum computing, can have a significant impact on artificial intelligence in healthcare. It is crucial to design AI solutions that can be adapted and scaled while guaranteeing safety and sustainability throughout their implementation.

To meet the challenges of adoption, it is advisable to adopt a multidimensional approach that involves ongoing research and collaboration between the various players involved. The aim of this strategy is to improve the integration of AI into clinical practice while preserving rigorous ethical standards. A focus on collaboration between healthcare experts and technologists will further enhance the responsible use of AI, leading to improved outcomes for all patients. See references: (Elendu et al., 2023; Mennella et al., 2024).

References

Bouderhem, R. (2024). Shaping the future of AI in healthcare through ethics and governance. *Humanities and Social Sciences Communications*, 11(1), 1–12. https://doi.org/10.1057/s41599-024-02894-w

Dash, S., Shakyawar, S. K., Sharma, M., & Kaushik, S. (2019). Big data in healthcare: Management, analysis and future prospects. *Journal of Big Data*, 6(1), 1–25. https://doi.org/10.1186/s40537-019-0217-0

Dhirani, L. L., Mukhtiar, N., Chowdhry, B. S., & Newe, T. (2023). Ethical dilemmas and privacy issues in emerging technologies: A review. *Sensors*, 23(3), 1151. https://www.mdpi.com/1424-8220/23/3/1151

Dwivedi, Y. K., Kshetri, N., Hughes, L., Slade, E. L., Jeyaraj, A., Kar, A. K., Baabdullah, A. M., Koohang, A., Raghavan, V., Ahuja, M., Albanna, H., Albashrawi, M. A., Al-Busaidi, A. S., Balakrishnan, J., Barlette, Y., Basu, S., Bose,

I., Brooks, L., Buhalis, D., & Carter, L. (2023). "So what if ChatGPT wrote it?" Multidisciplinary perspectives on opportunities, challenges, and implications of generative conversational AI for research, practice, and policy. *International Journal of Information Management*, 71, 102642. https://doi.org/10.1016/j.ijinfomgt.2023.102642

Elendu, C., Amaechi, D. C., Elendu, T. C., Jingwa, K. A., Okoye, O. K., John Okah, M., Ladele, J. A., Farah, A. H., & Alimi, H. A. (2023). Ethical implications of AI and robotics in healthcare: A review. *Medicine*, 102(50), e36671. https://doi.org/10.1097/MD.0000000000036671

Farhud, D. D., & Zokaei, S. (2021). Ethical issues of artificial intelligence in medicine and healthcare. *Iranian Journal of Public Health*, 50(11), i-v. https://doi.org/10.18502/ijph.v50i11.7600

Gerke, S., Minssen, T., & Cohen, G. (2020). Ethical and legal challenges of artificial intelligence-driven healthcare. *Artificial Intelligence in Healthcare*, 1(1), 295–336.

Jeyaraman, M., Balaji, S., Jeyaraman, N., & Yadav, S. (2023). Unraveling the ethical enigma: Artificial intelligence in healthcare. *Cureus*, 15(8). https://doi.org/10.7759/cureus.43262

Li, Z., Koban, K. C., Schenck, T. L., Giunta, R. E., Li, Q., & Sun, Y. (2022). Artificial intelligence in dermatology image analysis: Current developments and future trends. *Journal of Clinical Medicine*, 11(22), 6826. https://doi.org/10.3390/jcm11226826

Mennella, C., Maniscalco, U., Pietro, G. D., & Esposito, M. (2024). Ethical and regulatory challenges of AI technologies in healthcare: A narrative review. *Heliyon*, 10(4), e26297–e26297. https://doi.org/10.1016/j.heliyon.2024.e26297

Olawade, D. B., Wada, O. Z., Odetayo, A., David-Olawade, A. C., Asaolu, F., & Eberhardt, J. (2024). Enhancing mental health with artificial intelligence: Current trends and future prospects. *Journal of Medicine, Surgery, and Public Health*, 3(3), 100099–100099. https://doi.org/10.1016/j.glmedi.2024.100099

Oluwafemidiakhoa. (2024). Revolutionizing medicine: How quantum computing and AI converge in the next healthcare paradigm. https://medium.com/kinomoto-mag/revolutionizing-medicine-how-quantum-computing-and-ai-converge-in-the-next-healthcare-paradigm-c8cfc680bc07

Overgaard, S. M., Graham, M. G., Brereton, T., Pencina, M. J., Halamka, J. D., Vidal, D. E., & Economou-Zavlanos, N. J. (2023). Implementing quality management systems to close the AI translation gap and facilitate safe, ethical, and effective health AI solutions. *NPJ Digital Medicine*, 6(1), 1–5. https://doi.org/10.1038/s41746-023-00968-8

Rasool, R., Ahmad, H. F., Rafique, W., Qayyum, A., Qadir, J., & Anwar, Z. (2023). Quantum computing for healthcare: A review. *Future Internet*, 15(3), 94. https://doi.org/10.3390/fi15030094

The Future of AI in Healthcare - Treatment, Diagnostics, Ethics, Challenges in Software Development. (2024). https://selleo.com/blog/the-future-of-ai-in-healthcare-treatment-diagnostics-ethics-challenges-in-software-development

Wang, C., Zhang, J., Lassi, N., & Zhang, X. (2022). Privacy protection in using artificial intelligence for healthcare: Chinese regulation in comparative perspective. *Healthcare*, 10(10), 1878. https://doi.org/10.3390/healthcare10101878

Yelne, S., Chaudhary, M., Dod, K., Sayyad, A., & Sharma, R. (2023). Harnessing the power of AI: A comprehensive review of its impact and challenges in nursing science and healthcare. *Cureus*, 15(11). https://doi.org/10.7759/cureus.49252

Index

Printed in the United States
by Baker & Taylor Publisher Services

Printed in the United States
by Baker & Taylor Publisher Services